THE WAR TRAIL
OF BIG BEAR

*Being the Story of the connection of
Big Bear and other Cree Indian
Chiefs and their followers with the
Canadian North-West Rebellion of
1885, the Frog Lake Massacre and
events leading up to and following it,
and of Two Months' Imprisonment
in the Camp of the Hostiles*

BY

WILLIAM BLEASDELL CAMERON

SMALL MAYNARD & COMPANY
BOSTON, MASS.
1927

Printed in Great Britain

BIG BEAR.
CHIEF OF THE PLAINS CREES.

CONTENTS

LIST OF ILLUSTRATIONS

CHAPTER I

It fell in the quiet night,
* There was never a sound to ken ;*
But all of the woods to the right and the left
* Lay filled with the painted men.*

STEVENSON

THE FROG LAKE SETTLEMENT

Four hundred miles east of the great continental backbone of North America, the Rocky Mountains, and six miles north of the North Saskatchewan River, a collection of substantial log buildings in the year 1885 had reached the dignity of a small civilized community known as the Frog Lake Settlement.

The Saskatchewan is the grand river of the old Canadian North-west Territories. Rising in the Rockies, it flows east, draining most of that immense sweep of hill and plain, forest, lake and muskeg through its connections into the broad Arctic reservoir of Hudson Bay. Like Mississippi, Saskatchewan is a Cree or Algonquin word and means "Swift-running." During many years steamboats sweated their way fifteen hundred miles up the tortuous channels of the main stream and its two chief branches, the North and South Saskatchewans, with merchandise for Fort Edmonton, then a trading centre of the Hudson's Bay Company, now the capital city of Alberta, and slipped back on its hurrying flood with peltries in rich packs on their way to the world's fur market at London.

Frog Lake, for many years following 1885, as a place of human abode no longer existed. It fell back into the embrace of that wilderness from which it was once in part wrested. The mystery of silence brooded over it. The pilots of its first feeble steps toward an ordered progress slept beneath its grass-topped hillsides, and ashes covered the ground whereon stood their habitations. The traveller passed quickly along the trail leading through it and camped at night away from its sombre associations. Even the savage author of its desolation shunned a spot where in the dark his unquiet fancy conjured up the accusing shades of stunned and martyred victims. For on the morning of April 2nd in that year of 1885 the red man whose home this wilderness was arose with his fierce blood galloping in his ears and casting aside his dissembled amity, struck to the earth the intruder upon his heritage.

That paleskinned stranger had come boldly upon the land as though it had belonged to him. True, a treaty had been made, but he did not regard the gods, the traditions or the customs of its people. He scoffed at the wisdom of its chiefs and prophets. He treated them not as equals and brothers but as children, foolish, untaught. He would have shown them a new manner of life. They cared nothing about any new manner of life; they were satisfied with life as they knew it. Except that they had thought that life would have been easier, somehow, after the treaty was signed.

At first had they made him welcome, sharing their meat and camp fire according to the ancient usages of the red peoples. Then for a time they had marvelled and endured and spoken in secret council. And at length when the opportunity arose they had thrown off the mask of submission to the new order of things that had come uninvited upon them and rifle and torch in hand sped to the work of vengeance and destruction.

It is the story of the Frog Lake Massacre I have to tell. There is nothing pretty about it. A stain dark and bloody on the page of Canadian history, that is all it is. Yet as history it is worth preserving. I lived at Frog Lake, was present at that massacre and narrowly escaped the fate that overtook my luckless fellows. For months afterward the unexpected report of a gun put my heart in my mouth. In my dreams painted savages raced yelling after me at early dawn through belts of dark firs, over knolls, across valleys; bullets sang in my ears or buried themselves in my flesh; and I awoke gasping and unable in the first seconds of consciousness to convince myself that it was not all a horrible reality. Even after all these years I do not often care to dwell in memory upon that dreadful time. But always I have felt that it would one day be my part to set down faithfully what I knew and saw and it is in that feeling that this is being written.

Fortunately I am not dependent on memory alone, which might prove fickle. Copious notes concerning the events, preserved from the time of their occurrence, afford a basis for confidence and make the work comparatively easy. The story is a plain one and I shall endeavour to tell it plainly. Neither is there place in it for much play of imagination, and if the dramatic setting, the romantic atmosphere of a wild and lonely land, the smoke of tepees and the native eloquence of men naked and brown as leaves in autumn, which are inseparable from the bald and simple narrative, do not invite the devourer of the sensational and melodramatic in literature the tale is not for him.

A few words at the outset respecting the country and the various bands of Indians inhabiting it will simplify my work and anticipate the necessity for hindering explanations in the body of the narrative.

The settlement of Frog Lake consisted of three main groups of buildings—government, Hudson's Bay Company and Roman Catholic mission; the store of a trader named George Dill, and a small grist mill in course of construction.   There were the dwellings of the Indian agent, farming instructor, interpreter, the North-west Mounted Police barracks, stores, blacksmith shop, stables and outhouses; the Hudson's Bay Company's trading shop, store, dwelling and stable; the mission church and dwelling.   The mill and residence of its builder, John C. Gowanlock, lay some two miles nearer the Saskatchewan than the main settlement, located at the foot of Frog Lake, a beautiful sheet of water fifteen miles in length, connected with the Saskatchewan through a creek bearing the same name.

The settlement was in the centre of a reservation of several square miles belonging to three bands of Wood Cree Indians.   On this reservation, within a radius of three miles, were scattered the houses of the Wood Crees.   The region is rolling and diversified.   Small lakes sleep in the hollows between the hills; the prairies are interspersed with bluffs of poplar, willow, birch and spruce.   Feathered game, rabbits and fish abound; deer, moose and fur-bearing animals are also plentiful in the vicinity.

It was due to these natural advantages, combined with the rich soil, that the land had been chosen by the Wood Crees as a home for themselves and their families.

The Cree nation is divided into two branches which, speaking practically the same language, differ widely in character and mode of life. The Plain Crees are better orators, more active, warlike, crafty and savage than their Wood Cree brethren. Big Bear and Poundmaker were both Plain Crees, though Poundmaker was elected a chief only a few years before the rebellion, while Big Bear was an hereditary chief and bore the reputation of having as a young man been the bravest warrior among the Crees. Big Bear was rather short of stature for an Indian and of stronger and more compact build than the ordinary red man. His chest was enormous. He had a large head, thick neck, broad forehead and small cunning deep-set twinkling black eyes. His nose was long and prominent, the nostrils thick and strong, his lips thin and straight and his chin and jaw square and powerful. His general appearance was that of a resolute politic savage and born leader of men.

The Plain Crees were the hereditary enemies of the Blackfeet. Their territory was the great plains between the North and South Saskatchewans, where in bands and mounted they hunted buffalo, fought their battles and whence they made predatory excursions into the countries of neighbouring tribes.

The Wood Crees, on the other hand, were a race of solitary hunters and trappers afoot. They lived in the wooded country north of the North Saskatchewan and seldom ventured on the plains among their more warlike brethren. They were the backbone of the fur trade in the Saskatchewan country and had for years lived at peace with white traders and missionaries. They had acquired some skill in agriculture, which they followed when not engaged in their regular business of trapping furs. The Indian is always a beggar and the Wood Crees possessed this characteristic along with the other tribes.

Still farther to the north, stretching well down toward the Arctic Ocean, lay the territory of another race of fur hunters, the Chippewyan or Athabascan family of tribes.

Having now distinguished the different nations having a place in this narrative, I may begin my story.

CHAPTER II

THE ANNUITY PAYMENTS AT FORT PITT

It was October, 1884, and the Plain Crees of Big Bear's band were camped above the North Saskatchewan River near Fort Pitt. The Indians were assembled to receive their annuities, which would be paid at Pitt on the 20th of that month. Under the treaty the chiefs received each twenty-five dollars, councillors fifteen, all others—men, women, children—five dollars each every year " while grass grew and water ran."

Fort Pitt was an old and important trading-post of the Hudson's Bay Company, thirty-five miles from Frog Lake. George Dill and I had made the round of the payments at the various reservations with a trading outfit in competition with other traders for a share of the Indians' crisp new notes. Now our tents were pitched near the Indian lodges in readiness for the business that would follow the last and largest payment, that to Big Bear and his band. The Indian's day of affluence is soon past; his money is gone almost as soon as he receives it.

A new prophet and champion had arrived among the band. I had met Little Poplar at Frog Lake a few days before. He had come from Fort Pitt with an order on John Delaney, the farming instructor, for provisions. I learned later how he had secured it. On the trail he had encountered the government inspector of Indian agencies. The following dialogue ensued:

Little Poplar: " Who are you ? "

Inspector: " Me ? I visit the reservations every year to see that the Indians are properly treated, that they have what is necessary. I'm an inspector."

Little Poplar: " Huh ! That's what I am, too— an inspector. I come from the country of the Kitchemokomanuk (Americans—Long-Knives); I wanted to know whether or not my people were well treated. They are hungry, I find. Give me a *musinagen*—I want thirty sacks of flour, ten sacks of bacon, tea, sugar; that will be good medicine. Quick ! "

He got the order. I was standing with Delaney in front of the agency when Little Poplar drove up with his Crow brother-in-law. He was a handsome Indian. Above medium height, straight as a rush, muscular, with clean square-cut features, full jaw, long plaited black hair, a quick tongue and cool aggressive manner, it was apparent at once that he was a savage bound to be a leader among his people and that a white man to deal with him successfully would have to possess exceptional tact and courage. He wore a fancy green blanket, leggings profusely beaded, moccasins, a wide leather belt with a heavy knife and Colt's revolver stuck in it, a broad Stetson hat encircled by a brass band and eagle plumes, brass earrings and brass bands on his wrists. Without mention of the order he stepped up to Delaney and said curtly:

" I want thirty sacks of flour, ten of bacon, ten pounds of tea and fifty pounds of sugar."

Delaney looked at the impudent savage with some curiosity.

" I don't know you," he said. " You may be in

treaty and again you mayn't. We don't give stuff
even to treaty Indians whenever they take a notion
to ask for it. To strange Indians and non-treaty
Indians we don't give anything at all."

Little Poplar's lower lip stuck out. "Why
doesn't the Big Chief Woman send agents who can
do something? It is men like you"—he looked
insolently at Delaney—"that cause trouble between
the Indians and the police like they had at Poundmaker's last summer!"

He drew from under his blanket the inspector's
order and handed it to Delaney. "Now, am I
going to get the provisions?" he sneered.

Of course he got them. Delaney could not refuse,
though he was plainly nettled. The supplies were
loaded on the carts that had trailed Little Poplar
and he returned to Pitt. T. T. Quinn, the Indian
agent, followed a day or two later with the cash
for the payment to Big Bear's band—which brings
me back where I began.

Little Poplar has been introduced thus early in
order to show the class of men who led what had
long been recognized as the most turbulent and
warlike band of savages in the Canadian North-
west, and because his influence and that of other
chiefs served to foment the discontent and restless-
ness in their followers which was so soon to culminate
in one of the most sanguinary events in the history
of the Canadian government's relations with its
Indian wards.

On October 19th Agent Quinn sent word to
Big Bear that he would pay the band at the Hudson's
Bay Company's post in the morning. The Indians
arrived promptly. They filled the office in the big

B

fort building where Quinn was seated; they packed the hall, the stairs, the doors and the open windows and trailed away into the square between the building outside.   All were painted and carried guns under their blankets.

Little Poplar was first to speak. He had come, he said, from across the line; come to see his people, do something for them. He had heard that they were hungry. That was so. The Americans treated their Indians better—gave them more to eat, more clothes. He would not speak much now. He would hear the others. After that he would speak.

Wandering Spirit, war chief, spoke next. He lamented the disappearance of the buffalo, the red man's one friend, and the Indians' destitution, contrasting it with the abundance of the past. Other leaders followed, speaking in the same strain.

Then Little Poplar rose again and walking out in front of Quinn, said:

" Are you Kapwatamut ? "

Quinn raised his eyes. " That's what they call me," he replied.

" May I look at you ? " the Indian went on.

Six and a half feet tall, spare, athletic, broad-shouldered, exceedingly active, Thomas Trueman Quinn was a splendid figure of a man. A native of Minnesota, notwithstanding his mixed Sioux and Irish-French blood he was well educated, exceptionally intelligent and had served with distinction in a Wisconsin regiment through the American Civil War. Afterward he had seen many exciting adventures while employed as a scout with the regular army in frontier Indian campaigns. It was from his knowledge of the Sioux language

that he received from the Crees his name of
Kapwatamut or The Sioux Speaker.

He rose leisurely, turned completely round
before Little Poplar, sat down again. He looked at
Little Poplar. " Seen all you want ? " he asked.

The Indian scowled. " I have heard of you ! "
he retorted. " I heard of you away over the other
side of the Missouri River. I started to come this
way and the farther I came the more I heard.
You're the man the government sent up here to
say ' *No !* ' to everything the Indians asked you ! "

Little Poplar bent over and shot the last sentence
at Quinn like a slug from a catapult. There was
intense silence in the room. The agent signed to
him to proceed.

" Now, I am going to ask you something. I
will ask it three times before I sit down. It is long
since the buffalo went away, my people are hungry
and would like to eat fresh meat again. Will you
kill an ox before the treaty money is paid ? "

Quinn shook his head. " The government gives
cattle to the Indians for work and milk, not to
kill. There's no beef for you."

Little Poplar went on: " I crossed the line and
travelled north. By and by I came to where the
grass had been torn up. Two iron lines had been
laid down and stretched away east and west as
far as I could see. (The Canadian Pacific Railway.)
I said to myself, ' What is this ? ' I thought for
a moment and then I said: ' *Hai*, yes; I know !
This is the *pewabisko meskano*, the iron road that
the government has built to carry food and clothing in their big wagons to the poor starving Indians.'
And I want them to bring money out the same way,

in the big wagons, and to throw it out on both sides of the iron road so that everybody can have plenty of it ! "

He turned to Quinn. " For the second time, I ask: Will you give us beef ? "

" I've answered that question. You heard what I said," replied the agent.

" Very well ! " Little Poplar raised his voice. " We will have the government build a telegraph line from here to Battleford, and "—he lifted the whip in his hand—" I will lash the wires as they do and we will have him removed ! I will have a new man sent in his place within a moon. I know the government has given orders that you are to have beef, but he won't follow them. I look around me," he went on, " and of all the leaders who stayed when we went south, how many are left ? I see one old man ! " He placed his hand on the white head of Chief Keehewin; then faced the agent: " For the third and last time I ask—and when you answer, *speak loud* so that every Indian in this house can hear—Will you give us beef ? "

" *No !* " came the reply in the deep voice of the agent. Little Poplar wheeled about.

" Go ! " he shouted, raising his arms. " Let him keep his *peecoonta* money ! *Neeuk !* "

And with yells of defiance the whole band swept out of the house, across the square and up the hill, firing their guns in the air as they went.

That afternoon the Indians danced the war dance and Big Bear made a speech. He attacked the government and the Hudson's Bay Company and ignoring the other whites present, walked up to Captain Francis J. Dickens, son of the novelist, commanding the North-West Mounted Police at Fort Pitt, and held out his hand.

"You are a man," cried Big Bear, "whom Manito made to be a chief! We like you; your heart is good. As for that man "—he pointed at Quinn—" his heart is made of stone! He may go back to Frog Lake. When the governor made the treaty with us we were told we should have beef to eat at every payment." He placed his hands, fingers extended, on either side of his head and turned fiercely on the agent. "You want my head—*take it!*" he cried, flinging his open hands in the agent's face as though delivering it to him.

"When I am hungry this winter and ask for food," said Miserable Man to Quinn, "if you don't give it to me I will kill you."

Quinn smiled good-humouredly. He had heard Indians talk before. He did not mind such trifles as their threats.

Big Bear apologized later to everyone for his harsh words, but for two days the band danced the war dance and refused to be paid. The police detachment was kept constantly under arms in anticipation of trouble and Quinn sent his half-breed interpreter to notify the chiefs that unless they came to terms he would return the following afternoon to Frog Lake.

Meanwhile the Hudson's Bay Company officer, having made large advances to the band, grew anxious about his debts. He ordered a steer to be slaughtered and sent as a gift to the Indian camp.

This mollified the Indians; still, they objected, the beef had not come from the government. They would compromise matters, they said, by accepting the money at their camp instead of at the fort. Quinn decided to humour them and sent word that he would pay them there next morning.

During these days of "strained diplomacy" Dill and I had nothing to do but mind our tent-store, fry our bacon, watch the Indian youngsters' deft archery and try otherwise to kill the time while awaiting developments. The Indians did not molest us. They came, talked, examined blankets, knives, print, shawls, handkerchiefs, rings—all our stock, but without money they could not buy. We were glad to hear a truce declared.

At eight-thirty next morning two troopers came with the pay-tent and pitched it about a hundred yards from our quarters. They were followed in twenty minutes by Quinn, who notified Big Bear by messenger that he was ready to begin the payment. The band was in council. After waiting for some time, Quinn walked over to our tent.

"In twenty minutes it will be ten o'clock," he said, looking at his watch. "If they don't show up before then they get no money."

He returned to the pay-tent. A little later he passed our place carrying under his arm a box sealed with red wax. It contained the annuity money—seven thousand dollars.

He had scarcely disappeared in the direction of the fort when Big Bear, Wandering Spirit, Little Poplar and other chiefs came rapidly toward our tent. They were talking excitedly and stopped a moment to ask what had become of the agent. We told them he had got tired waiting and had probably gone to dinner. Gesticulating angrily and with exaggerated expressions of amazement,

BIG BEAR TRADING AT FORT PITT, 1884.

(The Group includes Four Sky Thunder, Okemow Peeaysis (Big Bear's third son), Stanley Simpson, Louis Goulet, Corpl. Sleigh and Billy Anderson).

they went on. They overtook him before he reached the fort and persuaded him to return and make the payment.

For the next two days I was busy at the store. The Indians danced and feasted and I went once or twice at night with Stanley Simpson to the dancing lodge and heard Little Poplar count his *coups* and tell how, using me occasionally, and not altogether to my liking, as he swung his heavy Colt's pistol in my direction, as representing the enemy, he had taken Blackfoot scalps. Then Dill went to Battleford, ninety miles away, to deposit our funds and bring back a fresh stock of goods, while I returned to Frog Lake and put up a log building for our winter trading quarters. Soon after Dill's return, by mutual agreement we dissolved partnership. He continued what had been our business and I accepted a position with the Hudson's Bay Company at Frog Lake.

CHAPTER III

LET me go back a step to the reservation, on the Battle River south-east of Pitt, of Chief Poundmaker, where Big Bear was then in camp, and relate a happening there three months earlier that throws a yet more significant light on the attitude of these Indians than the events just recorded. I did not witness this, being a few miles away, and I am indebted to Major Fred A. Bagley, a veteran of the N.W.M.P., and to Mr. William McKay, of the Hudson's Bay Company, both of whom were active participants on the ground, for the details of what at more than one critical juncture threatened to end in a bloody debacle.

Kahweechetwaymot, a member of Big Bear's band, went to John Craig, farm instructor on the reserves of Chiefs Poundmaker and Little Pine, and asked for provisions for a sick child. The government furnished supplies to be issued when the need was evident to sick and destitute Indians, but Kahweechetwaymot did not get any. This was hardly surprising to anyone knowing Craig and the Indian. The one was a phlegmatic easterner; the other a pestiferous and not particularly intelligent savage. Anyway, Craig was doubtless following instructions—the Indian did not belong on Poundmaker's reserve—though some of the more politic of the government's agents were wise enough on occasion to forget them.

24

Kahweechetwaymot went off, but he was back in no time. With two aides. One was his brother. The other was a well-seasoned hickory axe-helve.

With these reinforcements, Kahweechetwaymot had no difficulty in obtaining all the provisions he required, which was considerably more than he would have been satisfied with in the first place. Craig arrived at the police barracks in Battleford some hours later, sore from the top down, inside and out, and gave Kahweechetwaymot a very bad name. Superintendent Crozier of the N.W.M.P., commanding at Battleford, sent Corporal Sleigh to bring in Kahweechetwaymot. He wanted to explain to him that the Queen felt much annoyed because of his course in instituting a self-administered code of rewards and punishments.

The Indians were holding their annual Thirst Dance on Little Pine's reserve—making braves. They were there in hundreds, many from distant points. It was a big fête. Kahweechetwaymot was taking a prominent part. His prestige was high. On the strength of his recent disciplining of a white farming instructor, he was by way of being regarded admiringly by the young men at the dance as an example of the real thing in braves.

Kahweechetwaymot scoffed at Sleigh. In fact, backed by public opinion in the form of the assembled tribesmen, he affected an indignant astonishment. How, he asked, was it that a policeman had the nerve to come there thinking to put him under arrest ? " Go back," said he to Sleigh, " and tell the Big Police Chief what I said."

Sleigh sent a man to town to report and Crozier realized that the situation was one demanding the personal attention of the Big Police Chief. It was beneath the dignity of Poundmaker and his fellow chiefs, he concluded, at such a time to discuss matters of any moment with his subordinates.

So at an early hour next day, Crozier appeared with twenty-five men—of whom Bagley, then a sergeant, was one—at Poundmaker's. They brought with them an Indian, met on the trail, who appeared entirely too ingenuous to be at large.   Once they were safely in camp on the reserve, he was liberated. As a matter of fact, he was a spy, sent out by Poundmaker to learn what the police were doing, as Crozier had guessed.

The tents up, Crozier took the police half-breed interpreter, Louis Laronde, and one or two troopers and went to the Thirst Dance camp, three miles away, demanding to know why Poundmaker and the other chiefs had refused to deliver up to his men Kahweechetwaymot, who had offended the Queen by striking one of her servants with an axe-helve.

Poundmaker temporized. He was a most deliberate and dignified personage. He told the big police chief not to be hasty. The sun would not go out; it was still high. It was best that matters of this sort be dealt with in calm discussion.

So all day long, while the big drum boomed and ambitious young braves skewered through loops cut in their chests rawhide thongs reaching to the top of the big centre-pole of the Thirst Dance lodge, flung themselves frenziedly backward in efforts to break their fleshly bonds and prove worthy to be counted warriors, and while other young men capered round on horseback, singing and shouting war-cries, Poundmaker and his brother chiefs gravely discussed the offence and the offender, while the police chief fumed and fought to control his temper.

The outcome of the deliberations was a compromise, the chiefs agreeing that at about noon next day they would produce Kahweechetwaymot for trial if court were held, not at Battleford, but at a plateau some four hundred yards from the position in which the police had made their camp. The selection of this site was a manœuvre engineered by the police officer to bring the negotiations under the guns of the improvised fort he intended throwing up.

Following the parley, Crozier dispatched a courier to Battleford, thirty miles away, with instructions to Inspector Antrobus to come with speed and all available men remaining in barracks to Poundmaker's. A little later Crozier and his force departed for the government warehouses on Little Pine's reserve, adjoining Poundmaker's six or seven miles to the west.

These warehouses contained all the stores, bacon and flour chiefly, on the two reserves. Crozier was decidedly against these stores falling by any chance into the hands of the Indians in their present mood. With four loaded ox-teams he started back to his camp at Poundmaker's.

The Thirst Dance camp straddled the trail, part of the four or five hundred lodges being pitched on either side of it. To avoid the Indians, Crozier detoured to the north of the trail with the wagons.

The Indians were watching him. When opposite the camp a hundred young bucks, mounted and

singing, burst suddenly upon him, circling the
wagons and firing their guns over the heads of the
little force.   The idea of the police marching off
with the provisions did not please them.   Doubtless
they had had these in mind themselves.   The
position was an uncomfortable one, but the police
ignored the warlike demonstration staged for their
benefit and marched on.   At dusk they reached the
camp at Poundmaker's with their loads.

Here were some old log buildings.   The men
were tired, the night was suffocating, the mosquitoes
were a plague and the commissary had fallen down
on its job—without the wagons they would have
had little to eat—but there was to be no rest for
the little company.   Crozier ordered all buildings
but one to be torn down.   Of the logs so obtained
he directed the construction of two rough bastions,
abutting on the remaining building.   The night
dragged but toward morning the job was finished,
the sacks of bacon and flour had been piled in tiers
behind the log walls to serve as breastworks and
the weary men stretched themselves on the ground
for a few minutes' sleep.   The completed fort was
in this form:

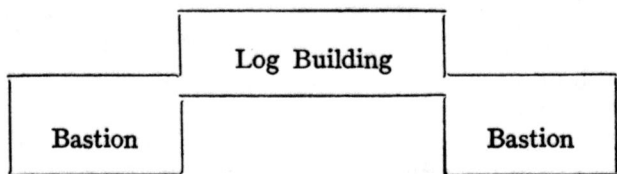

A deep slough behind the fort afforded protection
from that quarter.

Inspector Antrobus and Sergeant-major Kirk
with the reinforcements, totalling some sixty men

and including a number of Battleford civilians, reached Poundmaker's about eleven o'clock next morning and shortly after noon Poundmaker and his fellow chiefs arrived in accordance with their agreement at the plateau. Crozier assigned ten men to each of the bastions and leaving the others to await orders, covered by the twenty rifles and taking with him Interpreter Laronde, Constable Campbell Young and another man, went out to meet the chiefs and try Kahweechetwaymot.

Just a month previous the Crees had held a begging dance in the town of Battleford. Those old aboriginal dances were novel and spectacular; they interested us and we all—the whole town, or most of it—looked on. Poundmaker, wearing a breechclout and a vest studded with brass nails, his long legs streaked with white mud, on his head a small cap formed from the dried skin of a bird, was there. Big Bear was there, mounted on a white horse, a rusty black coat on his back and a battered black soft felt hat on his head. The old chief rode up and down before the stores, proclaiming loudly to the world at large that it was "*meewasin*" ("good") here, at Battle River; that it was not "hard" here, when the traders brought out sacks of flour, sides of bacon, packages of tea and sugar and thick plugs of tobacco and piled the gifts on the ground beside the dancing warriors.

Inspector Antrobus came past, riding a tall police horse. Imasees and Okemow Peeaysis, sons of Big Bear, bursting suddenly out of the crowd of dancers, galloped furiously across the prairie directly at the inspector. They carried in their hands folded umbrellas. As they reached Antrobus they jerked

their ponies to a stand and the umbrellas flashed
open. The police horse snorted, swerved violently,
the officer's pith helmet rose in the air and sailed
away over the grass and his startled mount bolted
wildly with him for the barracks.

The Indians, looking on, grinned delightedly.
Evidently they regarded the incident as a rattling
fine joke. The inspector on the contrary could see
nothing at all humorous in it.

An hour later the dance was over and the Indians
had gone to their camp on the hill south of the Battle
River, when Inspector Antrobus, accompanied by
William McKay, manager for the Hudson's Bay
Company at Battleford, appeared among the lodges
asking for the head chief. Poundmaker indicated
Big Bear. The inspector was intensely angry; he
trembled with rage.

" I have not much to say," he announced wrath-
fully, " and my message is for the head chief alone.
Let no one else speak." He turned to Big Bear.
" What are you doing here ? You have no business
in town. Unless you are packed and on the trail
back to the reserves in half an hour, I will put you
chiefs under arrest and lock you up."

Amazement for the moment held the Indians.
Then Poundmaker, his dark face flushing, jumped
to his feet.

" There will be a bullet here," he declared loudly,
a hand on his throat, " before you arrest one of us !
When we are ready we will leave; not sooner."

An old man got up. " He says no one must speak
but Big Bear ! " he cried. " Well, I am speaking.
Let him stop me ! Look at him," pointing at the
officer's legs. Their unsoldierly shaking must have

been mortifying in the extreme to Antrobus, who was anything but a timid man, but he could not stop it. Rage exacts its penalties. " And he tells us this ! " The old man snorted contemptuously. " '*Wus !* "

The Indians looked and once more they laughed at the inspector. Antrobus was beside himself. He could not trust his tongue to further words. He climbed into his buckboard and clattered off.

Two hours passed. ' The Cree camp was still on the hill south of the Battle, but no arrest had been made.

When Crozier went out to meet the chiefs, there was still some difficulty he found about Kahweechet-waymot's trial. The Indian, backed by the young men, declined to give himself up. They were all wild, said Poundmaker, and it was hard to do anything with them. At another time it might be done, but, Poundmaker pointed out, their pride revolted against a surrender in the face of such a great gathering of their people, many from distant reserves. So the unending talk went on. The police seemed to be getting nowhere. The prestige of the scarlet-coated upholders of the law was at stake. If they gave way it would be many a day before it could be completely regained. The last would never be heard of it. So long as an Indian present remained alive, he would boast amid the acclaim of his listeners about the camp fire at night of the time they bluffed the police.

Crozier's patience was exhausted. He quitted the council abruptly and returned to the fort.

William McKay had arrived from Battleford

about noon.   The McKays had been Hudson's
Bay Company officers for generations.   They had
been given by the Indians the family name of
Little Bearskin.   They were known to every Indian
along the Saskatchewan.   A Little Bearskin to these
Indians was a man to be trusted.   The McKays
possessed their confidence.

Poundmaker rose.   " I am going to the fort,"
he said.   " If I can prevent it there will be no
bloodshed.   Since this man will not give himself
up, I will offer to take his place."

Big Bear ran after Poundmaker.   " *N'chawamis*,"
he cried, " you will not be left to face the danger
alone.   If you go, Big Bear goes also."

Together the chiefs entered the fort, but came
out a moment later.   Crozier would not accept a
substitute, they told McKay; he would take only
Kahweechetwaymot.   The three seated themselves
on the grass before the fort to smoke and endeavour
to find a way of surmounting the difficulty.   Crozier
sent a messenger to McKay, asking him to detain
the chiefs.

" Tell Major Crozier I'm no policeman.   If he
wants the chiefs let him hold them himself," was the
Hudson's Bay man's answer.   He was not pleased.

Big Bear was taking little part in the discussion.
He watched the fort.   Suddenly he exclaimed:
" Something is going to happen.   Look ! "

The police had emerged.   They were buckling
on their sidearms and saddling their horses.   Poundmaker rose hurriedly.

" If there is to be trouble, my place is with my
men," he declared, and followed by Big Bear he
ran back up the slope.

The police advanced slowly, the sun flashing on their polished carbines, their scarlet coats aglow. They lined up before the Indians, a soldierly and formidable-looking company. That they could be relied on to give a good account of themselves was not to be doubted.

Sergeant Bagley had been assigned to one of the bastions. He glanced over at the corral, and saw " 'Andsome 'Arry," the solitary remaining horse, Bagley's trooper.

" You're in command here," he told the corporal beside him ; ' I'm resigning," and disregarding orders he slipped over to the corral, mounted and joined the line out in front.

Crozier confronted the tall chief, to whom the Indians were looking as their spokesman. This was his land; Big Bear was taking no prominent part. At the officer's request, McKay acted as interpreter.

" Poundmaker," he announced, " I came out for this man and I am going to take him."

The Indian thrust out his long face. His black eyes kindled, passion shook him and Bagley, watching, saw him strike, seemingly unconscious of what he did, with the sharp points of the knife-blades in his pukamakin, at his right leg. Blood welled out and flowed down the legging. His cloak of friendliness, for apparently it was a cloak, fell away and he stood revealed, a hostile among the hostiles.

" He won't be given up ! " he declared vehemently, stamping his foot. " You say you are going to take him ? " He lifted a tapering forefinger and tapped his chest. " Take me first—if you dare ! "

Antrobus stood near. He glanced at the chief

c

and passed a slighting remark. It was not understood by Poundmaker but he guessed its import.
He was infuriated. He had not forgotten the
inspector or his threat at the begging dance the
month before. He lost for the moment his accustomed restraint. Raising his pukamakin, he rushed
upon Antrobus. The three knife-blades in the end
glittered above the officer's helmet.

"Redcoat dog!" he hissed.

But Constable Prior poked his carbine in the
tall chief's face and the deadly pukamakin dropped
slowly to his side.

Suspense gripped the Indians. A deep hush
had fallen. Now the reaction came. The excitement
rose to an uproar.

"Plenty blood will be spilled on the banks of
the Cut Knife to-day!" shouted Imasees.

Some minor chiefs, peaceably disposed, appalled
by the impending explosion, rode among the mob,
waving green branches, imploring the aggressors
to be reasonable, to consider before it was too late.
Their example had some effect; the storm sank
to a murmurous undercurrent. But in a moment
it rose again, more violently than ever. The hostiles
surged round, jeering, whooping, raising their guns
threateningly, goading the police with taunts and
epithets.

Wandering Spirit, who in the war dance counted
thirteen Blackfoot scalps, rushed out and seized
McKay by the wrist, endeavouring to drag him over
to the Indians' side.

"Come!" he urged frenziedly. "You are
crazy. You will be killed!"

McKay pulled away.

Little Pine, amiable and friendly always, sitting his horse, addressed the mob. They were wrong, he told his people, to defy the police. He was a notable chief, a warrior as well as an orator of parts, and he spoke forcibly and at some length. But they heard him with impatience. They had reached the stage where pacific words were almost an offence. Little Pine died shortly after the trouble. Rumour had it that poison was responsible ; that he paid with his life for the stand he took that day in opposing the more turbulent among the bands.

Sergeant-major Kirk sat like a statue on his horse in front of the line, gazing stonily ahead. At his horse's muzzle stood Wandering Spirit, muscles tense, dark eyes agleam, thin lips working, his lean claw-like hands gripping a Winchester. When the din was at its peak, Bagley saw the Indian strain and lift as though struggling under some ponderous weight and the rifle came up. Bagley held his breath.

"Now it's coming ! Now old John's going to get it ! "

The words said themselves over and over in the sergeant's mind.

The blood-lust burned in the war chief's eyes, dull red pools glowing murkily in their sultry sockets. The seconds passed. What was restraining him ?

The sullen tide beating against the tough barrier that had so far contained it—the counsel of leaders able and tried, accustomed to being deferred to— might at any moment burst through. The pressure of a finger, red or white, against a trigger and a flood would descend that would drench that sunlit slope in waves of crimson death.

It was as if the war chief were stretched on a rack of conflicting emotions—the hunger to kill that was his consuming passion and a foreboding that made him pause. Should he be the one? Dare he take upon himself that sinister responsibility? Did he see confronting him the vision of a day of reckoning some time to come, a day when the white man would exact the ultimate price?

The old police warrior never flickered an eyelash. And when the lull came the rifle was lowered again. Bagley breathed once more. Then came the renewed uproar and again the menacing rifle lifted.

Miserable Man rode round behind Kirk. " I will fight with the police ! " he declared loudly. But he had no intention of fighting on the side of the police. Miserable Man was a dissembler. His purpose was to make sure that, between himself and Wandering Spirit, the sergeant-major should not escape. To take the scalp of an officer would be greater glory than to tuck under his belt that of an ordinary policeman.

An Indian rode over to the depression on the left of the police line. " Keep quiet, there ! " Bagley heard him say. And it came to the sergeant then that all along he had been conscious of a droning murmur of women's and youthful voices and he sensed the grim menace that lurked in the wooded hollow.

The clamour fell and rose once more and once more the threatening rifle of the war chief came up. But again it came down unfired. Why, as will be evident before this narrative is ended, is an eternal riddle.

Crozier turned to Laronde. " Which is him— the man we want ? " he asked.

A tall Indian, a sneer on his evil face, Cree words of contempt on his lips, danced and cavorted in the van of the mob. The interpreter pointed.

"That's him." And as the Indian, noticing, dived suddenly among the others: "There he goes!" he added.

McKay called to him and the Indian came out. Said the Hudson's Bay Company officer:

"Tell the police okemow you will surrender. You will get a fair trial. You may be punished but they can't hang you. If trouble starts the police will not be the only ones to suffer. Many of you will die also. Do you want to see that? Be a man! Give yourself up!"

"I won't!" returned Kahweechetwaymot surlily.

Twin Wolverine, Big Bear's eldest son, pushed his horse into the police line beside Constable Campbell Young. "I am going to fight against you!" he shouted to his fellow-tribesmen. Unlike Miserable Man, the Twin Wolverine meant what he said.

McKay turned to Crozier. "Arrest your man," he advised.

"Think we'd better do it now?" queried the officer.

"Yes. The longer it is put off, the greater the danger. There has been too much talk already."

"The two men afoot on the right, fall out and seize that fellow!" came the command.

Kahweechetwaymot wheeled to run. "Nab him!" McKay prompted Laronde. The interpreter rushed and seized Kahweechetwaymot. The two policemen followed. Before the Indian realized how it had all happened, Constable Warren Kerr

—" Sligo " to the force—had Kahweechetwaymot
by the long plaits of his black hair and had landed
him with a swing that had nothing gentle about it
among the policemen on foot. They closed about
the prisoner and his captors.   The horsemen
quickly encircled them and the whole body began
to move off, the men in the rear facing backward
with their carbines ready for instant action.

McKay paced evenly up and down between the
two rows of levelled rifles.

Bedlam broke loose.   The Indians went wild.
" Shoot them, shoot the red coat dogs ! " they
howled. " Why do we wait ? Now—*now* was the
time we agreed on to wipe out the dog *chemoginusuk !* "

But the cooler men among the redskins frantically
fought the outcries of the hotheads. " No—*no !
Be careful ! Wait !* Let the red coats shoot first ! "
And, referring to McKay, walking coolly up and
down between the opposed forces: " Shame !
Would you kill a Little Bearskin ? "

They brushed past the Hudson's Bay official
and charged the retreating ranks, jostling the men,
snatching at their clothing, stabbing their horses
with the points of their knives, hoping to stampede
them.   One man, cut off from the others, was
stripped, his tunic and sidearms forcibly appropriated.   Poundmaker himself wrested away his
carbine.

But the horses, like their riders, held firm.
And no Indian fired.   Neither did a policeman.
Because the police, disciplined and obedient to
orders, could not and would not under no matter
how aggravated provocation, be first to breach

the peace.   But if, even by accident under the tension, a single shot had sounded——!   What would have followed, no man present during those pregnant moments cares to contemplate.

Maddened over the successful coup of the police, a dozen of the most truculent braves seized Laronde and, powerful though he was, rushed him off through the poplar bluffs.   That he, a half-breed with their own blood in his veins, should have aided the enemy—that, above all, he should have pointed out to the police okemow, and later stopped Kahweechetwaymot—incensed them beyond anything else.   Laronde's chances of living seemed exceedingly remote.

The police flung their horses against the ring of passion-distorted faces and at length pushed through and reached the fort.   The Indians crowded them, with jeers and epithets, to the walls.   Kahweechetwaymot was shoved through an opening into the waiting hands of the men inside and the police followed.   The Indians stormed about outside.

McKay drew Major Crozier aside and spoke to him in an undertone.

" Throw out the bacon and the flour ! "

The men doubted whether they had heard aright.   Pull down their defences, their breastworks ?   He could not mean it.

" Throw out the bacon and flour ! "   There could be no doubt about the command this time.   " Look alive, men ! " the commandant added.

The heavy sacks went over.   The effect was magical.   The angry clamour died.   The camp was a huge one, its food supply scant.   The Indians were hungry.   In the surprise of sudden abundance they forgot their quarrel with the redcoats. They pounced upon the sacks, each struggling to secure a share before he was too late. The women and boys came from their place of concealment and joined their men in the raid. They lugged the stuff off through the bluffs to their lodges. The suggestion had been McKay's and his strategy was a winner. He knew Indian character.

And while the Indians, unheeding, fought over the spoil, the police bundled a most subdued and crestfallen brave into a wagon and in half an hour were on their road with him to Battleford.

After all an Indian, take him by and large, is nothing but a grown-up child.

Laronde turned up as they were leaving. Again McKay had intervened. "Let him go!" he had insisted. "Don't blame him; he's paid to do this work. That's how he makes his living. If you want a prisoner, why don't you take the police okemow?"

McKay knew that he was safe in making what at this stage was a perfectly impractical suggestion.

Before the police left, McKay hunted up Poundmaker.

"You must surrender the rifle you took from the policeman," he told him.

Poundmaker's quick temper flared again. "I will not!" he exploded. "He was going to use it against us!"

"Now, see here." McKay talked patiently to the handsome red man as he might have done had he been explaining some puzzling matter to an angry boy. "You must not look at this thing in that way. The gun did not belong to the policeman. It does not belong to the police at all. It belongs to the Queen."

Poundmaker pondered this. Three years before he had guided the Marquis of Lorne, Governor-General of Canada, three hundred miles across the plains from Battleford to the Blackfoot Crossing. Poundmaker was an unusual Indian. He was the typical chief as one has been accustomed to picture him from the literature of his youth—tall, dignified, deliberate in speech and manner, his striking face framed in a setting of raven-black hair hanging in two immense plaits far below his waist, with a certain native air of courtliness and distinction that impressed all who met him. No wonder that Lord Lorne had made much of the stately red man. Perhaps that was why Poundmaker held the governor-general in some respect. He did not wish to displease the noble lord's mother-in-law, the Queen. So in the end the gun was surrendered.

Half a dozen of us, civilians, were on our way from Battleford to Poundmaker's reserve. The parley out there had lasted for three days. We had heard in Battleford that the situation was critical. The addition of a few rifles might be acceptable to the police, we thought.

The afternoon was intensely hot. We had off-saddled half-way out to breathe our labouring horses and enjoy the poplared shade and clear cold water of Medicine Drum Creek. A horseman hove in sight, coming from the direction of Poundmaker's. He came up.

" The fun's all over, fellows," he told us. "They're on their way in with their man. You might as well go home."

In this and the preceding chapter I have endeavoured to show Big Bear's band in a characteristic attitude of hostility to the government. The leaven of mischief was already at work; they were prepared to start, with all the inherent cruelty of the savage, on a course of rapine and bloodshed at the first favourable opportunity. How soon that opportunity was to arise the handful of white men who had made their way into that primitive corner of the far North-west beyond the Saskatchewan could then have small conception.

CHAPTER IV

WHEN in the year 1875 the Saskatchewan Indians met the commissioners appointed to treat with them for the cession of their rights, the only chief of importance to refuse the proposals made by the government was Big Bear. Acceding probably to the demands of the more unruly element in his following, he gave as a reason his objection to the white man's law which permitted hanging. He also wished, he said, to see how the promises made to the tribes would be kept by the government.

The action of Big Bear in thus declining to subscribe to the document surrendering his country and his liberties to the white man's dominion gathered about him the independent spirits among his people and he soon came to be recognized as the most powerful chief of the Cree nation.

While the buffalo continued plentiful the band lived much as they had done before emissaries had come from the Big White Mother to buy their heritage. They became a band of nomads and drifted south, across the line into Montana. The buffalo, mercilessly hunted for their robes by white men, soon disappeared; Big Bear and his followers became a menace to the ranchmen of the treasure state and were driven back into Canadian territory. Reduced to the extremity of want and wretchedness, in 1883 at Fort Walsh Big Bear at length affixed his mark to the treaty.

But though they had come into treaty, Big Bear's band obstinately deferred following the example of the others and selecting a reservation. They excused their tardiness on the plea that there were so many fine locations it was hard for them to agree on a choice. Thus while reservation Indians when in need—as often happened—got help from the government, for Big Bear there was no such provision. During the first winter—1883-4—they did as a matter of fact get a few supplies from the Indian agent, but this was in payment for work done. With the advances they received from the Hudson's Bay Company on account of their treaty money and furs and game they killed, they managed to live through the winter.

The following summer, as has been seen, found them at Poundmaker's reserve, where the incident just related—the flare-up precipitated by the ruffianly Kahweechetwaymot—occurred. Shortly after this affair Big Bear's band returned to Fort Pitt for the payments already described, and this brings the story to the winter of 1884-5. During the spring of 1884 while trading on my own account among the Saskatchewan reservations I had spent some time at Frog Lake. I was, therefore, no stranger to these Indians when I returned the following New Year to take up residence in their territory in a new capacity.

The months of January and February passed uneventfully. Big Bear and his band were camped in the timber along Frog Creek not far from the mill site. They cut wood for the police detachment, freighted for the Hudson's Bay Company and got some occasional help from Indian Agent Quinn.

The old chief often had dinner with me; thus I had frequent opportunities to study his deeply-lined, intelligent face. Big Bear was then perhaps sixty years of age. He had an amazing voice and when he talked, as he often did, with his right arm free and the left holding the blanket folded across his broad chest, with the dramatic gestures and inflections natural to him, he reminded me of an imperial Cæsar and was one of the most eloquent and impressive speakers I have ever listened to.

On my trips to Pitt during this period I spent several days with Mr. W. J. McLean, chief officer of the Hudson's Bay Company for the district, and his hospitable family. We played cards, danced, sang, took snowshoe tramps, organized rabbit hunts. I made the round of his trapline across the big river from the fort once or twice with Stanley Simpson and helped him to bring in seven foxes.

About March the first rumours reached us of impending trouble between the government and the French half-breeds at Duck Lake. Louis Riel, who had incited the rebellion among these people in 1870 and been outlawed for his action, was again their leader. We had, in fact, known earlier that half-breed runners from Duck Lake had visited Big Bear's band, but had not anticipated any serious outcome. The half-breeds claimed their title in the country had never been extinguished and professed to believe they were to be dispossessed of their land holdings. They were ripe for hostilities and sought the co-operation of the Indians.

Andre Nault, a French half-breed cousin of Riel, was arrested at Fort Pitt while on his way early in March from Duck Lake to Frog Lake and detained, on suspicion of being the bearer of incendiary messages from Riel to Big Bear, for several days by Captain Dickens. On being liberated he boasted openly that he would soon be in a position to revenge himself on the police. How successfully the rebel Riel, through specious promises, had drawn Big Bear's lawless followers into a league with him against the whites was shortly to appear. The half-breeds had a logging camp at Moose Creek, twenty miles west of Frog Lake. I have always believed that Nault was a Riel spy.

CHAPTER V

On the evening of March 28th I closed the trading shop early and with my skates under arm, walked over to Frog Creek, intending to skate down to Gowanlock's. Gowanlock lived in a house near the dam, with his wife and a clerk named William Gilchrist.

The weather had been mild for some days and there was much water on the ice. I had not skated two miles before I was thoroughly wet and decided to go ashore and walk back to the settlement.

The trail took me through Big Bear's camp. The band was in council. The smoke-blackened tops of the lodges stood among the naked poplars, through the ugly, swinging limbs of which the raw north wind swept in fitful gusts, soughing dismally. Underneath, the rumpled snow softened in the first clasp of spring. The stars hid behind the cheerless grey curtain of clouds overhead. In and out between the lodges slunk stealthy, starving curs, snapping viciously at one another over bones long picked clean.

I noticed the tense, serious looks on the faces of the warriors smoking the long stone pipe round the fire in its centre as I entered the lodge. I saw at once that this was no ordinary social affair. I pulled once or twice at the pipe when it came to me in its course round the circle and I heard and understood enough, though the talk—in the Cree

47

tongue—was guarded, to make it clear that subdued excitement burned in the breasts of the Indians —that they were contemplating some eventful step.

The talk was of " news." Wandering Spirit, the war chief, rose and spoke earnestly in his low, impassioned voice and with that transfixing look in his dark eyes that I have never seen in those of any other Indian. Then he drew his shirt over his head and presented it to Longfellow, brother to a Wood Cree chief. Longfellow followed, and he in turn handed his shirt to Wandering Spirit. And all the while the calumet of compact continued to pass from mouth to mouth round the circle. Big Bear's band, it was evident, was making proposals of some kind to the Wood Crees.

Big Bear was away, hunting in the mountains to the north of Frog Lake with his two sons. Little Poplar, with his family, was at Battleford.

I knew all the Indians well, for I had met them almost daily at the trading post during the winter. But I saw that I was not altogether welcome and I soon left. As I walked home through the slush in the dull and lonely night, I had a premonition of evil days at hand and I felt uneasy and depressed.

It was three days later that we got the " news " the Indians evidently were expecting. I strolled into the mounted police barracks at eleven o'clock at night and found Constable Billy Anderson just arrived with the report of the half-breed rising at Duck Lake. He had ridden the thirty-five miles from Fort Pitt in a little over three hours, through the darkness and the melting snow, across the slippery, hilly country, and his horse streamed sweat. He had brought dispatches from Captain

Dickens for the corporal in charge of the Frog
Lake detachment, R. B. Sleigh.

The police at Fort Carlton and the Prince Albert
Volunteers, said the dispatches, had met the rebels
under Riel and Dumont and after a sharp engagement been compelled to retreat, with a loss of
thirteen men killed and many wounded.   The
Captain suggested that the Indian agent and the
other white residents at Frog Lake should come
into Fort Pitt. He added that he was ready to come
with his men to Frog Lake, however, if we thought
that the better plan.   The Fort Pitt garrison
numbered about twenty.

Anderson had brought mail for the settlement.
I was postmaster and walked over to the Hudson's
Bay Company's post to assort it.   Indian Agent
Quinn dropped in on his way to the Roman Catholic
mission to tell the priest.   He asked me to accom-
pany him.

"Well, Cameron, we'll be pulling out of here before
daylight.   I suppose you'll be ready?" he said.

I had not considered going, and I told him so.

"There's a lot of furs and stores on hand here.
My chief's at Pitt and I'm in charge. If he'd wanted
me to go in he'd have written.   I'm hardly at
liberty to leave without orders."

Quinn stopped abruptly and faced me. "Don't
be a fool, Cameron!" he exploded.   "You don't
know Indians as I know them. You're not obliged
to wait for orders to save your life."

His vehemence surprised me, but I answered
stubbornly: "If I felt like that about, I wouldn't
hesitate; I'd go. But I don't. These Indians aren't
going to kill me, whatever happens. I'm not trying

D

to influence anybody, though. Anyone who doesn't
feel safe should leave, I'm thinking."

Secretly, I hoped they all would leave. I should feel
safer alone with the Indians. And I smelled adven-
ture, something that appealed to me. I was young.
But as Quinn had said, I did not know Indians. I
only thought I did. I realized this a day or two later.

Quinn did not try further to persuade me and
we went together to the mission. Père Fafard was
in bed, but he came down and opened the door at
our knock. An old man named Williscraft, staying
with the priest, was present while we discussed
the situation and Quinn proposed to the priest
that we join the other whites and leave Frog Lake.

The missionary at once demurred. We should,
he said, show that we had confidence in the Indians,
now trouble was come.

Because, I suppose, he was a Roman Catholic,
the priest's views upset Quinn's own better judgment. " Oh, all right, Father," he said; " if that's
how you feel I'll stay too, though I did think that
to go to Pitt would be wisest for us all."

We went in a body to Delaney's. Besides the
farming instructor and his wife, Corporal Sleigh,
Mr. and Mrs. Gowanlock, Gilchrist and George
Dill were present. The question was debated anew.
Father Fafard again voiced his views, and at length
it was decided that, with the exception of the police,
we should all remain at Frog Lake. In view of the
recent reverse at Duck Lake and the known sympathy of the Indians with their kinsmen, the half-
breeds, while refraining from advising the others
as to their course, I advocated the departure of the
police. Six policemen would be no possible pro-

tection to us in the event of an outbreak against
the overwhelming numbers of the Indians, while if
Big Bear's band was evilly disposed they would begin
the trouble by picking a quarrel with the redcoats.
Sleigh was ready to go or to stay, as we wished.

Quinn agreed with me. "And, since you're
going, Corporal," he said, "I wouldn't lose any
time in getting away. If the Indians learned of it
—there's no telling. They might take it into their
heads to stop you."

I said to Sleigh: "I've two kegs of powder and
eighty pounds of ball over at the shop. It would
be as well out of the way. If you're not too heavily
loaded——"

"Sure," he said. "We can take it, all right."

He sent Constable Loasby with me and we
brought the ammunition to the barracks. I kept
a little powder and a few loose balls were left
scattered about the floor. I reasoned that if the
Indians rose and asked me for ammunition, it
would not conduce to their friendliness to be told
that I had none. Either they would suspect me of
lying or of having made away with it.

Just before daybreak a double police sleigh
slipped out of Frog Lake and disappeared among
the hills across the chain of lakes opposite. And I
had taken my last leave of Corporal Sleigh, as true
a gentleman as ever wore the Queen's uniform.

When I went to my room at the post to throw
myself on the bed for a little sleep, I glanced out
of the window. An Indian in a red blanket, rubbing
his eyes, hurried along the deserted road in the
track of the departed sleigh. Here was fresh
" news " for Big Bear's band.

CHAPTER VI

BIG-LIE DAY

At nine o'clock I was up again, had had breakfast and gone to the trading shop. It was the first of April. A Big Bear Indian came in. Wandering Spirit was at the farming instructor's house, he said, and sent word that Agent Quinn wanted to see me. I closed the shop and walked over.

Wandering Spirit grinned as I entered. He wore his war bonnet and seemed in excellent humour. " Big-Lie Day ! " he exclaimed. The other Indians present laughed. So did Quinn. I joined them. There were more dupes than one there, that first of April morning, and they were not the Indians.

Imasees, Big Bear's son, said to the agent:

" Sioux Speaker. We have had bad advice from the half-breeds this winter. They said they would spill much blood in the spring. They wished us to join them. They have already risen; we knew about it before you. They have beaten the soldiers in the first fight, killing many. We do not wish to join the half-breeds, but we are afraid. We wish to stay here and prove ourselves the friends of the white men. Tell us all the news that comes to you and we will tell you all we hear. The soldiers will come, perhaps, and want to fight us. We want you to protect us, to speak for us to their chief when they come."

Quinn replied: " You make good talk, Imasees. I am glad you wish to remain friends with us.

The fighting is far from here. Stay on the reservation and no one will bother you. I will see that
you do not want for food."

Miserable Man joked the agent about his threat
in the fall. They shook hands as they passed out.

" I'm glad Wandering Spirit seems friendly,"
remarked Quinn. " He has a great reputation as
a warrior among the tribes and as war chief is
most to be feared. So long as he stays quiet we
have nothing to worry about."

Perhaps it was because I came to know him so
well and witnessed the ferocity of his wild, complex
nature when roused, that Wandering Spirit has
always filled the first place in my memory among
the many Indian chiefs I have met. Tall, lithe,
active, perhaps forty years of age, of a quick,
nervous temperament which transformed him at
a stroke in moments of excitement into a mortal
fiend, he was a copper Jekyll and Hyde—a savage
no more to be trusted than a snake. An odd thing
about him was his hair. Whereas the hair of the
ordinary Indian is as straight as falling water, the
plaits of the war chief, while long and black like
any other Indian's, stood out about his head in
thick curls, forming a sombre background for his
dark, piercing eyes. And those eyes ! Shall I
ever forget them ? I can see them yet, in all their
burning intensity, flashing here and there, seeing
everything, as though it were yesterday. His nose
was long and straight, his mouth wide and lips thin
and cruel. He had a prominent chin, deep sunken
cheeks and features darkly bronzed and seamed
about the eyes and mouth with sharply-cut lines.
His voice was usually soft and intriguing; when he

spoke in council it rose gradually until it rang through the camp. It had a smooth, velvet quality that reminded me always, somehow, of the panther he so much resembled in other ways, and of its soft, caressing paw—with the claws of steel beneath the velvet.

" He was never much to steal horses," Four-Sky Thunder said to me one day later in the camp, when he called with a present of tobacco and we sat smoking in the lodge. " His greatest pleasure was in fighting, and he has killed more Blackfeet than any warrior among us, not excepting Big Bear."

First councillor, head soldier, war chief, cruel as the grave, a hunter of men, as proud of his record as any gold-laced general of his decorations —Kahpaypamahchakwayo, the Wandering Spirit.

In the evening I walked over to Quinn's house, dropping on the way into Delaney's. I found there Gowanlock and his wife, Gilchrist and Dill. They asked me whether Mr. Simpson, my chief at Frog Lake, had returned from Pitt and on my replying in the negative, jokingly remarked that he must be afraid to come out. I answered that if we all had as little to fear as my chief I should feel easier; he had known and traded with Big Bear and his band for twenty-five years and he and the old chief were great friends. I felt I suppose unreasonably irritated. Plainly these people did not sense the gravity of our position. It seemed to me no time for flippant talk. True, the Indians had not as yet given us cause for apprehension, but we were at the mercy of their every whim and who could say that a situation of deadly peril and anxiety might not develop at any moment ?

I went on to Quinn's. Crossing a ploughed field beside the house, I almost stepped in the darkness on an Indian. He crawled away at my approach. They were guarding the agent's house, then! He was not to be allowed to escape as the police had done.

Quinn was seated in his office, just off the front hall. Big Bear, Imasees and one or two others of the band were with him. Imasees gave me his chair, passing a common Indian joke about me, at which all laughed excepting Big Bear. The chief had returned that afternoon from his hunt. His striking face was dark and swollen from the cold and the smoke of many camp-fires and he looked weary and troubled. He was speaking of " Uneeyen " —Riel—the half-breed rebel leader, and went on:

" He said to me, ' Big Bear, much blood will flow.' He was trading whisky on the Missouri River and wanted the Crees to help him make war.

" When I was in the Long Knives' (Americans') country I had a dream, an ugly dream. I saw a spring shooting up out of the ground. I covered it with my hand, trying to smother it, but it spurted up between my fingers and ran over the back of my hand. It was a spring of blood, Kapwatamut ! "

Imasees left the house. His father's talk seemed to trouble him. The old chief rose. " Good night, Kapwatamut," he said. He extended his hand, and there was deep concern in his voice as he looked into the agent's eyes and repeated: " Good night ! "

After they were gone, Quinn said: " They seem friendly. Guess they're going to be all right."

I answered: " Something's troubling Big Bear; he behaves queerly. I'm sure no harm's to be anticipated from him personally.   I'd like to feel as sure of the others."

I remained with Quinn until eleven.   He told me of the Minnesota Massacre in the '60's, when his father, an Irishman and a noted scout for the United States troops, had been ambushed and killed by the Sioux.   Also of his own narrow escape at that time, when the hostiles at grey dawn raided the small frontier town where he was employed in a trading business and he had jumped in an empty barrel and worked it under the counter with his fingers.   The Indians had missed him when they sacked the store and he had got away that night.   Half starved, after several perilous days and nights he had at length reached a military post.   He said to me as I was leaving:

" Well, Cameron, they might kill me, but they can't scare me."

Poor Quinn ! I wonder if he guessed how soon his courage and his boast would be put to the proof ?

One Man and Sitting Horse, the uncle and brother of Quinn's wife, a Cree woman, went to him in the night with horses and offered to see him well on the way to Fort Pitt.

Quinn would not go.

CHAPTER VII

IN THE POWER OF THE HOSTILES

BIG BEAR, as I learned from him long afterward, went straight to his lodge when he returned to camp and went to sleep, for he was tired. Imasees, Wandering Spirit and other of the leaders were in secret council. At midnight the war chief gave an order and four of those in the lodge stepped out quietly and vanished in the gloom.

Isadore Mondion was a minor chief of the Wood Crees with a house on the reservation. He had Iroquois blood in his veins. His father as a young man had paddled his canoe from the St. Lawrence to the Saskatchewan, a voyageur in the service of the Hudson's Bay Company. Mondion was strong, intelligent and fearless and a friend of the whites. He did not care for these councils of Big Bear's band; no good was to be expected from them, he thought.

Soon after midnight the door of his house opened and four of Big Bear's warriors filed silently in. They seated themselves on the floor, and Mondion rose and extended the usual Indian hospitalities. He blew the dull coals in the mud chimney into a blaze and hung the copper pail over it for tea.

"The night is dark," he said. The visitors nodded. "It is warm." Yes, it was warm, Little Bear agreed. There was a long pause. "You visit late. For what do you come to see me?"

Bare Neck spoke. "Wandering Spirit sent us.

57

You are not a true Cree. Already the police have gone. He does not wish the other whites to leave. He does not trust you."

Mondion's eyes flashed. "Wandering Spirit is wise; also he is very brave, and he must think his followers very brave, too, that he sends four to guard a single man!"

Little Bear lowered his rifle threateningly. Mondion struck it up. They clinched and rocked back and forth across the room, until they went down, Little Bear under. The others drew knives and threw themselves on Mondion. They dragged him away and bound him. Not until near daylight did they release him.

Meanwhile Wandering Spirit had not slept. Spies lay about the agent's house. It was still dark at four o'clock when Imasees and Chaquapocase entered noiselessly through a window and crept upstairs to Quinn's room. His wife was awake and sprang out between the would-be assassins and her husband. Lone Man and Sitting Horse, her brother, flung into the room and confronted the others, guns in their hands.

"Dogs!" cried Lone Man. "Is not his wife a Cree woman and my niece? Let him alone!"

They departed, scowling. "Wandering Spirit will deal with you!" muttered Imasees.

Lone Man was brave and influential, a son-in-law of Big Bear.

"Who is Wandering Spirit?" he sneered. "Tell him Kapayagwan Napapowit protects Kapwatamut!" They remained in the agent's room. Soon daylight began to filter through the windows. Wandering Spirit forced the front door and entered the office. He took down the three guns hanging there.

"Kapwatamut !" he called. "Come down !"

"Do not go, Kapwatamut !" Lone Man urged. "We will stay and defend you."

Quinn laughed mirthlessly. "It is useless," he said. "And never will they be able to say Kapwatamut was afraid to face them !"

He reached the foot of the stairs to find himself surrounded. Wandering Spirit placed a hand on his shoulder. "You are my prisoner," said the war chief.

I was sleeping soundly in my room at the Hudson's Bay post. I awoke with a start. A hand, clutching my shoulder, was shaking me roughly. It was just sunrise. I sat up. Walking Horse, a Wood Cree employed about the post, stood beside the bed. His eyes were ablaze with excitement.

"*Waniska!* Get up !" he cried in Cree. "I think it will be 'bad' to-day !"

"What do you mean ?" I asked.

"They have taken the horses from the government stables, already," he replied.

"Who has taken the horses ?"

"They say, the half-breeds, but I believe it is Big Bear's men."

I needed no further urging. I dressed quickly and went down stairs.

Immediately, Imasees entered, followed by twenty of the younger bucks. Their faces were daubed with vermilion and they carried rifles. Usually the chief's son greeted me with some pleasantry, but there was nothing of friendliness on his unsmiling features this morning. He stopped in front of me.

"Have you any ammunition ? " he asked curtly.

I thought I was fortunate to be able to tell him that I had.

"Well, we want it."

He knew the regulations as well as I did. "Where is your order from the agent ? You can't get it without that."

He leaned forward, his face close to mine. "This is no time for idle talk ! If you don't give it to us, we'll break the shop open and take it."

My bluff had not worked. " Oh, if that's how you put it, I'll open the shop. If you're bound to have it I can't prevent you. I don't want the lock broken."

Opening the shop, I called my friend, Yellow Bear, behind the counter. "Hand that keg out," I told him. "I won't touch it."

I had, as has been seen, sent the bulk of the powder to Pitt with the police. They divided what I had kept—perhaps two pounds—among them. Miserable Man leaped over the counter, elbowed me roughly aside and gathered up the scattered bullets on the floor. Others reached across the counter and helped themselves to the long butcher-knives on the shelves, and files with which they began to sharpen them. Big Bear pushed his way in.

"Don't touch anything in here without leave !" he commanded sternly. " Ask him for it," indicating me with a wave of his hand. He left the shop again.

Yellow Bear stepped out among them. The old man scowled at the young bucks, shouldering them toward the door. "You have got what you wanted. *Neeuk !* Go !"

He closed the door and stepped back behind the counter. He picked up a muskrat spear. " I'll take this," he said. " I might want to use it. I have no gun." Big Bear's men had already secured all our weapons.

I was heartily grateful for the old man's friendship this 2nd of April morning. " Take anything you wish, Yellow Bear," I told him. " And whatever happens, stick to me."

We had in stock two boxes of Perry Davis's Painkiller. It contains alcohol and opium. I feared it might fall into the hands of the Indians and their ugly mood did not seem to need any stimulating. We took it to the house and hid it behind the chimney upstairs.

On coming down again, I found a messenger from Wandering Spirit awaiting me. I was wanted at the agent's house, he said. I went, under the guard of young men he had sent. They did not behave in any unfriendly manner; simply surrounded me.

There were nine white men beside myself in the little settlement, and when I reached Quinn's office I found them all seated in it. Quinn sat at the farther end with the Scotch-half-breed interpreter, John Pritchard, and Instructor Delaney near him. The Indians crowded round them and blocked the doorway. Wandering Spirit held the centre of the floor. He was speaking. His manner aroused in me a distinct feeling of dismay.

" Who is at the head of the whites in this country?" he demanded, shaking his fist in Quinn's face. " Is it the governor, or the Hudson's Bay Company, or who ? "

Quinn laughed. I think he must already have abandoned any hope that he would be permitted to see another sunset; the laugh was harsh and forced. It may have struck him as finely ironical that the men who made the regulations for the government of these Indians should be free to walk about securely in their eastern homes while he, an instrument in carrying them out, was a prisoner of these Indians and in danger of his life at their hands.

" Sir John Macdonald, a man at Ottawa," he replied. " He is the chief of all the white men who deal with the Indians."

The speech ended with a demand for beef. They were returning to their old form of attack on the government and the agent. Would he have the fortitude, now that he was at their mercy, to refuse ? Quinn turned to the instructor.

" Is there an ox on the reservation that has out-lived his usefulness ? " he asked carelessly.

Delaney mentioned one so old as to be no longer serviceable. Quinn said they might kill it and sent a Wood Cree boy to point the animal out.

The office was close, and the menacing attitude of the Indians and the way in which they hemmed us in no doubt made it seem closer. I felt extremely thankful, therefore, when upon gaining their point they permitted us to go outside and get a breath of fresh air. Some of Big Bear's men asked me to return to the shop; they wanted tobacco. Gladieu, a Wood Cree leader and my good friend, approached Wandering Spirit.

" Leave Cameron there," he told him. " You will be wanting other things."

The war chief, I knew against his will, agreed. I hardly need say I was glad.

I found Yellow Bear at the shop. " Stay close to me, and when they get what they want order them out," I said to him in a low voice as I unlocked the door. "They have the strong hand to-day, and I can't do it."

Afterward I went into the house and charged what they had taken—as I remember it, chiefly to the government. I know I felt at the time that the authorities were not without blame for the position in which we found ourselves. Quinn should have had a strong force of the police at his back when he was sent to deal with the most intractable band of Indians in the country.

Some of the Indians passed through the house as I was making these entries. They looked over my shoulder and asked what I was doing. When they were told, they laughed. Mrs. Simpson, wife of my chief at Frog Lake and herself a half-blood, watched me closely while the Indians were about. Evidently she feared for my safety. But I would not dwell on the dark possibilities; I could not think that they would cold-bloodedly injure those who had placed themselves unreservedly in their power, and I resolved to keep up as long as possible at least the semblance of authority.

Rev. Felix Marchand, missionary priest at Onion Lake, twenty miles on the way to Pitt, had arrived at Frog Lake the day before. He, Père Fafard, Henry Quinn, Yellow Bear and myself had breakfast together about nine-thirty in the Company's house. I say breakfast, but we had little appetite for food. We discussed our position and agreed that it was indeed grave.

Shortly after the priests left. An Indian woman, greatly agitated, entered the house. " Little Bear struck Père Fafard in the eye with the butt of his riding whip," she whimpered. Pessimism swept over me. Anything might happen now.

I went back to the shop. George Dill's store stood on a hill directly before the Hudson's Bay post. They had looted it early in the morning, breaking in the doors and windows.

Wandering Spirit dropped in. Since I had last seen him he had smeared his eyelids and lips thickly with yellow ochre. He looked hideous.

" Why don't you go to the church ? " he asked in his hard voice. " Your friends are already there."

No smile played on the face of the war chief to-day; instead, the worst passions of his savage nature were depicted there.

I was not a Roman Catholic, but I did not dare disregard what was in effect an order, and I walked over. On the way I met Four-Sky Thunder, one of Big Bear's councillors. He bowed, smiled and said: " N'Chawamis ! (My Little Brother !)" as he passed me. I felt grateful to the tall, pleasant warrior. The looks that Wandering Spirit had given me had been black enough.

The door of the church was open. Several armed and painted Indians stood before it. Father Marchand stepped down to close it, but Father Fafard stopped him. Big Bear and Miserable Man stood inside at the back. The chief told me later that he was there to prevent bloodshed and I believed him; for though outwardly calm, well do I recall the suppressed feeling and determination on the old warrior's face. I am convinced that Big Bear would have flung himself upon the first of his savage followers to point a gun and fought for our lives.

All the whites were assembled, as well as the half-breeds. The priests were celebrating mass, for it was a holy day of their church—the day before Good Friday.

I stepped across to the row of pews opposite the door and took a seat.

CHAPTER VIII

THE MASSACRE

THE congregation was kneeling.

A moment later Wandering Spirit entered. He wore his lynx-skin war-bonnet, with its five big eagle plumes, and carried a Winchester across his arm. He dropped on one knee in the centre of the church, resting the butt of his rifle on the floor. His eyes burned and his hideously painted face was set in lines of ferocious intensity. Never shall I forget the feelings his appearance excited in me, as he half-knelt, glaring up at the altar and the white-robed priests in sacrilegious mockery. He was a demon, a wild beast, roused, ruthless, thirsting to kill. I doubted then that we should any of us ever again see the outside of the chapel.

Prayers ended, the priests warned the Indians against committing any excesses and we were allowed to leave the church. The Catholics dipped their fingers in the water at the door and crossed themselves as they passed out. I returned to the shop and the other whites were soon after taken by the Indians back to the agency. King Bird, Big Bear's second son, accompanied me.

" *N'Chawamis*," he asked, " with whom do you side, Riel or the police ? "

" Cousin," I replied, " here we are all friends. The half-breed war is far from us. Let them fight it out between themselves."

He asked for the loan of the Hudson's Bay

Company's flag for the dance he said they intended holding later in the day.

Quinn, cool and self-possessed, his Scotch cap on the back of his head, his hands in his trouser pockets, dropped in on his way to the agency and we spoke together for a few minutes. Leaving, he said to me:

"Well, Cameron, if we come through this alive we'll have something to talk about for the rest of our days."

Wandering Spirit appeared in the door. "Go to the instructor's," he ordered, "where the other whites are!"

I complied. The Indians were sacking the police barracks. As I passed it, Yellow Bear came out, stopping me. Earlier in the day he had asked for a hat, but after thinking a moment had replaced it on the shelf, saying he would get it later. It was now ten o'clock.

"I want to get that hat," he said.

King Bird danced up to me, the Hudson's Bay flag over his shoulders. He shook with suppressed excitement. We had always been good friends.

"*N'gowichin!* (I'm cold!)" he said. He came closer and added meaningly, in a whisper: "Don't stop around here!"

I turned to Yellow Bear. "You can have the hat," I said. "Come with me."

He hesitated; the old man balked at missing his share of the police plunder. "Won't you bring it to me?" he asked.

"Wandering Spirit has just ordered me here," I answered. "If he saw me going back he might shoot me."

"Very well, then," said Yellow Bear; "I will go with you."

It was not much more than a hundred yards to the shop. Half way we met the war chief. He was running, carrying his rifle at the trail. He stopped and looked at me menacingly. "I thought I told you to stay with the other whites!" he cried.

Yellow Bear answered for me. "He is going with me to get a cap. I have none and the sun is strong."

Wandering Spirit considered. "Hurry back, then!" he said at length, and he ran on.

As I passed the Hudson's Bay house, I saw Big Bear talking with Mrs. Simpson in the kitchen.

Yellow Bear got his cap and I was locking the shop again, when Miserable Man appeared with an order from the Indian agent. I glanced across and saw Quinn standing on the hill I had just quitted.

I turn to an old scrapbook and from a piece of foolscap pasted in the back copy the faded lines, the last writing of my brave friend. It is worn and soiled, for I carried it in my waistcoat pocket for many weeks. It is undated, but to me nothing done on that 2nd of April needs a mark. It reads:

"Dear Cameron,
Please give Miserable Man one blanket.
T. T. Q."

Miserable Man was, I think, the most brutal-looking Indian I have ever seen. His face was deeply pitted by smallpox, and the yellow ochre with which it was coated made it appear even more repulsive than usual.

QUINN'S LAST WRITING: APRIL 12, 1885.

"I have no blankets," I said.

He did not reply, but stood regarding me doubt-fully with an ominous look in his rat-like eyes.

"What are you looking at him for?" demanded Yellow Bear. "Don't you hear him say he has no blankets? I know. They have even taken the blankets off his own bed."

Miserable Man was as great a coward as ever breathed. "Well, I suppose I can get something else." Yes, I told him.

"How much?"

"Five dollars."

He selected a shawl, a carrot of tobacco and some tea. I poured the tea into the shawl, as was our custom, and he was tying it up, when a shot rang out a short distance away. It was followed by two more in quick succession.

At the first shot the eyes of Miserable Man opened wide. He caught up the bundle and dashed out of the shop.

I followed, locking the door and putting the heavy brass key in my pocket. Two months later, on the day of my escape from the Indians, I left that key, hanging in a poplar bluff near Frenchman's Butte, in the pocket of a discarded pair of trousers. It was all that remained of the Hudson's Bay Company's business at Frog Lake. Perhaps some day a learned archæologist will discover it and write an interesting thesis showing how it came there and when, and deducing from the fact that they made locks and must therefore have lived in houses, additional proof of the high state of civilization of the mound-builders.

On the hill before the police barracks which I had

quitted ten minutes before lay the form of a man.
It was the lifeless body of poor Quinn. The air
was thick with smoke and dust. It rang with whoops
and shrieks and the clatter of galloping hoofs.
High over all swelled the deadly war-chant of the
Plain Crees, bursting from a hundred sinewy
throats. I heard Wandering Spirit shout to his
followers to shoot the whites, and crack after crack
told of the deaths of other of my friends.

" *Atim-eenawuk !* (Dog-men !)" exploded Walking
Horse savagely, but half-scared, looking out of the
Company's house. Big Bear rushed out of the kitchen
door and toward his followers, waving his arm and
shouting at the top of his voice:

" *Tesqua ! Tesqua ! (Stop ! Stop !)*"

He was too late. The smouldering fire of inherent
savagery had burst into flame and he was powerless
to quench it; the spring of blood of the old chief's
dream had broken forth and spurted through his
futile fingers !

My first thought was to seize an axe, lock myself
in the house and brain the first man to force the
door. But I looked about me and could see no axe.
An Indian raced up to me, holding his gun before
him.

" If you speak twice, you are a dead man ! "
he cried.

I saw a half-breed, Louis Goulet, run past, followed
by two Indians. One was his brother-in-law. He
was protecting him from the other. Goulet's face
was like paper. I turned to Yellow Bear.

" What shall I do ? " I asked.

The old man seized my wrist. His hand shook
as with the palsy.

" Come this way ! " he muttered, dragging me toward the scene of horror. But when he reached the corner of the house, he halted, glanced across and turned back. Big Bear's band had moved during the night and were now camped with the Wood Crees, a mile away. " No ! " said Yellow Bear. " These women are starting for the camp. Go with them; do not leave them. They will not shoot among the women ! "

Yellow Bear feared openly to befriend me—he would not accompany me—but I did as I was bidden, though I had little hope of reaching the Indian camp. I had gone but a short way when I met the Indian I had seen chasing Goulet. He was riding the half-breed's white horse, with his rifle across its withers. There was a fence on my right, making it impossible for me to avoid him. I drew back involuntarily, anticipating the worst. He raced up within six feet; then jerked his horse to a sudden stop. He eyed me narrowly for a moment.

" Go on ! Go on ! " he cried, then. " I don't want to hurt you."

I walked on. Mrs. Simpson looked off to the right in the direction of the firing. She began to tremble violently.

" Oh ! " she exclaimed, tears streaming down her face; " the priest has fallen ! "

I thought she was about to fall. I stepped back and caught her arm. She pulled away. " Run, white man ! " she cried in Cree.

" Do you think they will kill me ? "

" Run, white man ! " was her only answer.

I walked on. It was useless to run. Death staring

me grimly in the face ! That was what I saw.
Just that. Terrible ! I fixed my eyes on the ground
before me, held them there determinedly, momen-
tarily expecting the fatal bullet. I did not wish to
see when or whence it came. The sooner the better.
So I felt. It would be hard for me to describe my
feelings in those awful moments of suspense. I was,
I believe, resigned. I know I felt that it would be
a shame to live when so many of my friends were
being foully done to death a few short yards away.
I did not even look toward the spot where the
tragedy was passing. It seemed that if I did I
should be impelled to rush over and fall with my
luckless companions. To die without a chance to
defend oneself—therein lay the supreme horror !
Shot down like a dog ! If only I had a gun !

The moments passed. I still lived, and I took
heart and raised my eyes at last.

Other armed Indians were running on the ridges
near by. Two passed quite close to me. And at
length I reached the camp unharmed. I was told
to enter the lodge of a Wood Cree. The women
occupying it, all weeping, made tea and gave me
a cup. I felt sick and faint.

Soon I heard Wandering Spirit's voice. He was
striding up and down through the camp, speaking
in his ringing tones:

" *Kapwatamut nipahow !* (I killed The Sioux
Speaker !) I met him before the interpreter's
house. 'Kapwatamut,' I said; 'you have a hard
head. You boast that when you say no you mean no.
To-day, if you love your life, you will do as I tell
you. Go to our camp.'

" ' Why should I go there ? ' he demanded.

"'Never mind,' I said. 'Go.'

"'My place is here,' he answered. 'Big Bear has not asked me to leave. I will not go.'

"I raised my rifle. 'I tell you—*go !*' I shouted, and I shot him dead."

Three Indians entered the lodge and sat down near me. They looked at me curiously. I knew them well, but I did not speak. They had watches belonging to the murdered men. One, Papamakeesik, Père Fafard's murderer, held out a watch and asked me the time. It was eleven o'clock.

I groaned, sitting there, thinking over the horror. I expected each moment they would come for me. The suspense became unendurable. I could not longer rest with my fate undecided; I must go out ! I told these Indians. They were friendly enough to suggest that I disguise myself in a blanket, but I said no. I might be recognized. If I were I should be shot on suspicion of attempting to escape.

I walked across the camp into the brush. William Gladieu, the Wood Cree who had befriended me in the morning, followed with his gun. He put his arm about my shoulders.

"My brother," he exclaimed, "you are not to be killed. Before that happens they will walk over my dead body. Come."

He took me to the tent of Oneepohayo, head chief of the Wood Crees. Here a council was assembled. Yellow Bear, Little Bear, Gladieu and others, including the chief himself, spoke of kindnesses received at my hands—trifles as they seemed at the time, but which were to stand me in good stead now. They agreed that I should live and left me to secure Wandering Spirit's consent.

The Plain Crees were in council outside and the war chief made a speech to the band, instructing them that I was not to be harmed. They brought him to the lodge.

"This is the young man whose life we ask," said Chief Oneepohayo.

"Ah-ha !" answered the war chief. "He has done me favours too." He held out his hand.

Can anyone realize how sweet life really is until he comes near to losing it ? I doubt it. Mine, I began to think, might still be endurable—worth an effort to save. Though my spirit revolted I took the hand that had sped the bullets that sent two of my companions to a sudden and awful end, for besides the agent he had shot one of the priests.

"Walk about during the day as you please," he said, "but don't go out at night. You might be shot. One of the young men might do it and we wouldn't know who. And don't try to escape."

At Cold Lake, forty miles to the north, H. R. Halpin was in charge of the Hudson's Bay Company's post. A party was leaving to bring him to Frog Lake. I took advantage of their amiable mood to put in a word for him.

"Promise you'll spare his life, also," I urged. They debated the matter and made the promise. "So that he won't be surprised, I'll give you a note for him," I said, and on the back of an envelope I wrote in pencil:

"*Dear Halpin,*
The Crees have murdered every white man here except myself. They are going out for you and have promised not to harm you. At your peril, offer no resistance."

Beverley Robertson, the lawyer who defended

the Indians, had this note at the time of the trials, but I do not know where it is now.

Toward evening James K. Simpson arrived from Pitt. He was an old officer of the Hudson's Bay Company, with supervision over several posts and headquarters at Frog Lake, where I lived with him. As he drove into camp the Indians stopped his horses, unharnessed and appropriated them. He was an old friend of Big Bear and although a white man, in no great danger, for his half-breed wife had two sons members of the Wood Cree bands.

"Big Bear," said Mr. Simpson before the whole band, " I have known you for twenty-five years and I never thought I should live to see a thing like this ! "

There was deep feeling in the old chief's voice as he answered sorrowfully: " It is not my work. They have tried for a long time to take away my good name and they have done it at last. If you had been here, this might never have happened."

Mr. Simpson was allowed his own tent, while I was lodged with one of his stepsons, Louis Patenaude. I was deadly weary, and with the boastful jests of the murderers in my ears, lay down early and slept that night as soundly as ever I did in my life. It was a blessed relief to be able to forget in sleep the appalling events of that day.

These were the first hours of my memorable two months with hostile Indians.

I may here appropriately mention the fact that no servant of the Hudson's Bay Company was killed by the Indians during the whole of this stormy period. Their treatment by the Company had always been considerate and humane. If an Indian was sick he went to the nearest post and was supplied with food and medicine until he became well. When ready to go on a hunt he was outfitted with provisions, traps and ammunition, for which he paid in furs on his return. The Company made him advances in goods on account of his annuity and waited almost a year for payment, trusting entirely to his honesty for settlement of the debt. After a trade he always got a small present. When hungry he was never denied a meal.

It was this policy of liberality that created the bond of friendship that existed between the red men and the Company for more than two hundred years and of which they were not forgetful even in their moment of savage vengeance.

Yet the fact that I was an employee of the Hudson's Bay Company would not alone have saved me in that awful hour, and I cannot conclude this story of the massacre without recording here the sense of deep gratitude I shall always feel for life preserved under circumstances I can never cease to regard as anything but miraculous.

I have not yet mentioned Henry Quinn, the agent's nephew He was warned by the friendly Mondion some fifteen minutes before the massacre and escaped to Pitt.

CHAPTER IX

BESIDES James K. Simpson and myself, there were in the camp two white women, the wives of the murdered Gowanlock and Delaney. These unfortunate ladies were dragged from the bodies of their dying husbands by the savages and taken to camp, where they were purchased from their captors by John Pritchard, Quinn's half-breed interpreter, and another half-breed named Pierre Blondin. Pritchard deserves all praise for his unselfish and loyal part, for had the Indians retained possession of the women it is not difficult to divine the fate before them. A few words from their stories of the massacre will be found of interest. Mrs. Delaney says:

"The first we knew of the uprising was on the 2nd of April at five o'clock in the morning. Two of Big Bear's Indians entered our house and told us our horses were stolen by the half-breeds, though they were themselves the thieves. Soon after, some thirty more, armed and mounted, came to the house and forced their way in. They took all the arms and ammunition they could find, telling us they were short and required them. They said they wished to save us from the half-breeds. They took us first to Mr. Quinn's, where they had a long talk about holding together to keep back the half-breeds when they came to take the provisions. From Quinn's we were taken to the church, where mass was being celebrated, but they would not permit the priests to finish and ordered them to return with us to our house. We were left to ourselves for about an hour, the Indians surrounding the house. It was then about half past

77

nine in the morning. Big Bear came in and told my husband he feared some of the young men intended shooting the whites, but that he at least would be safe.

"A little later they ordered us all to go to the Indian camp. We departed, my husband and I with the others, taking only what we had on our backs, as we expected to be only a short time away. Before we had gone far the Indians began to shoot down the whites. Mr. Quinn was shot first, though I did not see him killed. All the shooting was behind my husband and me, and until otherwise informed I supposed it was into the air. I saw Mr. Gowanlock fall. As he dropped Mrs. Gowanlock leaned over him, putting her face to his. As two shots had been fired at her husband, I thought she had also been hit.

"After Mr. Gowanlock fell I saw some frightful object, an Indian hideously painted, aiming at my husband. Before I could speak he staggered away, but came back to me and exclaimed : ' I am shot.' He fell then. I called to the priest and he came toward me. Then the same Indian fired again. I thought the shot was meant for me, and I laid my head upon my husband and waited ; it seemed an age, but the ball had been for my poor husband and he never spoke afterward.

"Almost immediately another Indian ran up and ordered me away. I wished to stay, but he dragged me off, pulling me along by the arms through the brush and briar and through the creek, where the water reached to my waist. I was put into an Indian tent and left there until nightfall, when John Pritchard came and purchased my release with horses, and I believe both Mrs. Gowanlock and myself owe to him our escape from terrible treatment and subsequent death.

"I was terribly stricken down. I seemed demented and could hardly tell on one day what had occurred the day previous. I went on and on as in a fearful dream, but seemed conscious all the while of my home at Aylmer, and my longing for it seemed alone to keep me up. I was afraid to ask for my husband, but the half-breeds told me later that they had buried him.

"As I was being dragged away I saw the two priests shot. Father Fafard fell first ; then Father Marchand.

On four different nights Indians approached our tent, but the determination of Pritchard and some other half-breeds saved us."

The following is from Mrs. Gowanlock's story:

"When we left the Delaney's house no one knew what was about to happen and I do not think it was supposed any of us were really in danger. We all started at the same time. We had gone only a few paces when the Indians began firing. When I saw Mr. Williscraft fall in front of us I knew all were being killed and became greatly alarmed. I saw an Indian aiming at my husband by my side. In a moment he fell, reaching out his arms toward me. I caught him and we fell together. I lay with my face resting upon his and his breathing had scarcely ceased when I was forced away by an Indian. I was almost crazed with grief, but I remember seeing the two priests shot and Mr. Delaney. They were before me. One of the priests was leaning over Delaney. It all seemed like some horrible dream. I went through it dazed and stunned, with power enough left in my limbs only to follow, as the Indian dragged me after him through coarse brush and sloughs, which wet me through and tore my clothes and flesh. I must have suffered intensely, but grief and terror rendered me unconscious of pain.

" I asked to be put with Mrs. Delaney, but the Indian, who understood sufficient English to know what I meant, answered no and pushed me into his tent. The squaws inside noticed that I was shaking with cold and took off my shoes and dried them and offered me something to eat. Blondin came a little later and bought me for a horse and thirty dollars. I was then permitted to join Mrs. Delaney in Pritchard's tent. Like Mrs. Delaney, I dread to imagine the treatment to which we would have been subjected had it not been for Pritchard.

" Big Bear came frequently into the tent to see us. Pritchard would interpret and the chief professed sorrow, telling us it was the fault of his braves whom he could not control."

The unutterable sadness on the faces of these two poor women is ineffaceably stamped on my memory. We could offer them little beside our sympathy, and when I first saw them after the massacre I doubted if they would survive for a fortnight the fearful ordeal through which they had passed.

Nine men were killed in the massacre:

Thomas Trueman Quinn, a native of Minnesota, thirty-eight years of age, of mixed Irish, French and Sioux blood, successively interpreter, clerk and agent in the Canadian Indian service.

John Delaney, farming instructor, a native of Ontario, about forty years of age.

John C. Gowanlock, from Parkdale, Ontario, about twenty-eight years of age.

George Dill, about forty years of age. He came from Muskoka, Ontario, to Frog Lake in the fall before the massacre as my partner in a trading business.

John Williscraft came to the West from Southampton, Ontario. He was a mechanic, about sixty years of age.

William C. Gilchrist, clerk for Mr. Gowanlock, about twenty-one years of age.

Charles Gouin, a Columbia River half-breed, employed at Frog Lake building the agency stores and houses. He was about forty years of age.

Rev. Leon Adelard Fafard, a native of Quebec, where he was born in 1849.

Rev. Felix Marie Marchand was born in France in 1858.

In addition to shooting Quinn, Wandering Spirit was first to shoot Father Fafard. The priest was hit in the neck. He fell on his face, and Papamakeesik, who had been brought up by the priest, stepped out and finished him with a shot in the head.

FOUR SKY THUNDER (LEFT) AND OKEMOW PEEAYSIS
(BIG BEAR'S THIRD SON).

Facing p. 8o.

Dill and Gilchrist ran. They were followed on
horseback by Little Bear, Maymayquaysoo, Kahweechetwaymot, and Iron Body, overhauled and
shot down about three hundred yards away.

The bodies of the two priests and of Gowanlock
and Delaney were placed in the cellar beneath the
church and the earth walls thrown in upon them.
Quinn and Gouin were buried in the cellar of
Pritchard's house. Within a day or two of the
massacre all the buildings had been burned by the
Indians, including the two that were the sepulchres
of the murdered men.

The church was burned by Four-Sky Thunder,
who received a sentence of fourteen years for his act.

Apologists for the Indians—I listened to one
last summer; he had not been born at the time
the events regarding which he held forth transpired
—are fond of explaining that but for the obstinacy
of poor Tom Quinn there would have been no
massacre; that it was his refusal to comply with
the demand of Wandering Spirit and follow the
other whites to the Indian camp that drove the
war chief—already keyed to a high pitch of excitement—in a sudden burst of fury to loose the fatal
bullet. In other words, that the butchery was not
premeditated but the sequence to Quinn's insane
defiance of the fiery Cree leader at a critical moment.

This, no doubt, is a pleasant theory and I am
struck with admiration at the assurance of the men
who make it, but unfortunately it has no foundation
in fact, being built on entire ignorance of the
situation as it existed that 2nd of April morning.
I am as ready as anyone—more, I am *anxious* that
full justice be done the Indian and his many fine

qualities—but I am not prepared to hear without protest the blame for the tragedy placed on the shoulders of my good friend Quinn, who is past answering for himself, in order to bolster up a case for and excuse a lot of bloodthirsty and cowardly ruffians who were condemned by a majority of their own people.   Quinn knew Indians—he had good reason to know them, as will be evident to anyone who has been sufficiently interested to follow this narrative so far; moreover, he was himself part Indian, and if he declined to go to the Cree camp it was because he knew that if he were not safe on his own ground he certainly would not be safe among the Indian lodges.   It is my opinion that Quinn had satisfied himself these Indians were determined to kill him and decided that if he had to die nothing was to be gained by prolonging the suspense, meanwhile being exposed to their threats and abuse—of which I had seen something earlier in the day—until Wandering Spirit had worked himself up to the proper degree of ferocity to commit the dastardly act.

In view of these facts, therefore, I was pleased, long afterward, to get from Louis Goulet—who like myself was present at Frog Lake on that fateful day—the following details of happenings which did not come under my personal observation and which I should otherwise have had no means of learning.   They constitute a deeply-significant addition to what I myself knew and saw of the morning's proceedings, confirming my own conviction, not only that the massacre had been fully determined upon the night before if not earlier, but also that Imasees was its chief instigator and the war chief, if not his active abettor in its incitement, at least quite ready to assume the leading rôle in carrying it out.

Goulet's English being difficult of rendition in print, I give his story from the standpoint of an onlooker as it was told to me:

Goulet, Nolin and Nault had spent the night of April 1st at Frog Lake and next morning before sunrise they met at Gowanlock's, two miles below the settlement, on the way back to their camp at Moose Creek. Gowanlock and his wife were still up at the Delaney's and Gilchrist was alone. The half-breeds dismounted, tied their horses outside and entered. Gilchrist was up and they accepted his invitation to breakfast.

They were seated at the table, when the door was burst suddenly open and Imasees, an uplifted pukamakin in his right hand, rushed in. A look which he saw on the face of the chief's son Goulet interpreted as boding no good to Gilchrist. He sprang up and caught the Indian by the arms. Imasees swung his belligerent gaze on the half-breed and shouting, " You're the man I'm after ! " backed out of the house, dragging Goulet with him. A crowd of the young men of the band, armed and painted, stood about outside.

" Get on your horses and come up to Frog Lake," Imasees ordered. " You're not going back to Moose Creek. And bring the white man with you."

Goulet took Gilchrist up behind him on the saddle and the half-breeds started, the Indians trailing along in the rear on foot.

Presently the sun pushed a huge crimson shoulder above the skyline. It was a perfect morning.

" Ho ! " cried Imasees. " I like to see the sun get up that way—red, like blood. It's a sure sign of victory for the Indians, always ! "

Goulet turned to Nolin, riding beside him, and spoke in an undertone. " What's he talking about ? Who are they going to fight ? Victory ? What's he mean ? "

At the Roman Catholic Mission they were met by Wandering Spirit. He ordered them to dismount.

" I want you to interpret," said the Indian to Goulet. " Ask him "—he pointed to Gilchrist— " who he thinks will win, Riel or the government ? Whose side is he on ? "

Goulet put the question. Gilchrist laughed.

" The government, of course—I'm with the government. The half-breeds can't win."

" What does he say ? " queried Wandering Spirit. Goulet told him.

A sinister look swept the war chief's face. " That's all I wanted to know," he said significantly. " Come with me." And placing Gilchrist ahead, he stalked off.

(" The Indians liked Gilchrist," Goulet explained. " I suppose if he had said he sided with them they would have tried to spare him." It struck me that Goulet might have helped the white man here, but I expect he feared to give anything but a correct interpretation of his reply.)

The balance of his story I shall try to tell in Goulet's own words.

" Pretty soon," (said Goulet), " I meet Charlie Gouin. I say, ' Charlie, where's your rifle ? ' Charlie says, ' De Injin take it at my house, ' 'fore I'm up.'

"Well, dat don' look ver' good. Dere's goin'
be trouble, sure, I'm say to myself. And dere is.
You know how it go—at Quinn's office, at de
church, over on de hill 'front to Johnny Pritchard's
house. No use to tell 'bout dat. You been dere—
you see. Me, I'm t'ink I'm goin' 'scape away,
ba gosh ! But I'm never get de chance !

"Quinn an' Gouin's standin' 'front to Pritchard's.
Wandering Spirit's comin' up, order Quinn go on
de Injin camp. Dere's little patch de snow side
to de hill yet.

"Quinn take few steps; he's want to pass by
dat patch de snow. Wandering Spirit say, ' Go
straight ! ' Quinn go on roun'. Wandering Spirit
say: ' You always want go your way. Do w'oat
I tell you—go my way ! ' Quinn smile, keep on.
Den Wandering Spirit t'row up hees gun an' shoot
an' Quinn fall."

(Goulet's story here hardly corresponds with my
own. I think Goulet did not remember clearly
just what occurred at this time; I should be surprised if he did. He was alarmed for his own
safety, thinking of escape. My own account of
these details comes from the war chief himself,
from what I myself heard less than half an hour
after the massacre, when the murderer strode up
and down through the camp and I listened while
he cried out his own report of what he had said to
Quinn, the agent's replies and of what followed.
I scarcely think Wandering Spirit would have given
a wrong version of an event of which he was then
boasting.)

"Dat half-crazy feller you know," Goulet went
on, "run up, hol' his gun on me an' say: ' Give

me your money ! ' I'm say: ' I got no money.'
' Well, give me your horse,' he say. ' Quick.' I

"Of course, I give anyt'ing—dat—crazy feller
goin' killed me, sure ! 'All right !' I say.

"It's den I run on de pries' stable to get my
horse, Waychun runnin' 'long protect me, de time
you see me.

"But w'en I get on de stable, she's empty; an
Injin outside, he's sit on my horse. Dat's de same
feller's take Charlie Gouin's rifle; he got it on hees
hand. Well, I'm pretty—scare'. I'm run up, grab
dis feller on de leg an' give him swif' hois'. He's
land on hees head, odder side my horse.

"You bet dat feller's mad like — ! He's jump
up, swear de bes' he know how on Cree an' shove
hees rifle on my face. I'm get — close shave dere,
Cameron ! But Waychun step 'front to me—shove
hees gun on dat feller's face. So of course he don'
shoot. Dat's twice on few minute Waychun save
my life. I don' forget dat, you bet ! Many sack
flour I give Waychun after dat."

From there Goulet, still accompanied and protected by Waychun, struck for the Indian camp,
passing me on the way as already related, and it
was the "half-crazy feller," riding the half-breed's
horse, who halted me about the same time and
instead, as I anticipated, of shooting me, to my
unutterable gratitude, told me to "Go on !"

CHAPTER X

IN THE CRUCIBLE

On Good Friday, the day following the massacre, John Fitzpatrick, farming instructor at Cold Lake, fifty miles to the north, was brought into camp by Big Bear's runners. The Indians had been told by Riel that the Americans would send troops to assist them in their war against the Canadian government, and being an American, Fitzpatrick was looked upon as a friend.

King Bird put his head into Patenaude's lodge and said he had been sent by Wandering Spirit to summon me to the council sitting at the upper end of the camp. I had learned only too well what was likely to happen to anyone insane enough to disregard the war chief's wishes; I got up quickly and followed King Bird. As we walked along I said in Cree, with a wave of my hand in the direction of the smouldering ruins of Frog Lake:

" I hope there's going to be no more of *that* ? "

King Bird looked at me with his engaging frankness. " Oh, no," he answered. " Wandering Spirit wants only to talk with you."

It was a beautiful morning—the 4th of April. An atmosphere of peace, a melting, slumbrous haze, rested over all the virgin loveliness of that wilderness land—its wooded slopes, its sweeping green expanses, its soft blue lakes under the wide skies. It was hard to believe that amid such smiling settings there had been staged just two days before one of the blackest tragedies in Canadian history.

The council sat on the grass in a circle, a triple row of painted and befeathered savages. They made a way for me to reach the hollow space in the centre, and Wandering Spirit, who sat on his heels inside the inner row, motioned me to a seat beside him on the right. He wore his war bonnet and a rifle rested across his knees. From the bonnet depended five broad white eagle plumes, their points jet-tipped, for each of which I had heard him boast he meant to have a white man's life. Until then he had taken just two, those of Quinn and Father Marchand, so that three were still needed to make good his boast.

Immediately behind Wandering Spirit sat Imasees, half-brother to King Bird. Imasees was the real instigator of the Frog Lake atrocities, though clever enough so to manœuvre that upon others should fall the blame. He was emphatically a dangerous Indian—a cool, commanding figure in the flush of young manhood, with muscles of spring steel and the features of a Roman legionary. He wore his hair roached above his unwinking black eyes, like a horse's foretop, and he had about him something of the dominating force which despite his age still remained to Big Bear. In fact, so striking an example of the pure type of Plains savage was Imasees that notwithstanding his crafty and treacherous nature, I could not but confess a degree of secret admiration for him.

John Pritchard sat in the centre of the hollow space, with Mr. Simpson beside him. I noticed Fitzpatrick sitting with some half-breeds, including Andre Nault, Louis Goulet and Abram Montour, on the left of the circle. Louis Patenaude, my guard

IMASEES
BIG BEAR'S SECOND SON AND INSTIGATOR OF THE FROG LAKE MASSACRE.

Facing p. 88.

in camp, and Alexis Crossarms sat immediately
beside Wandering Spirit on the left; William
Gladieu on his right. The Plain Crees completely
surrounded us, As I walked to the place assigned
me and glanced over the banked ring of bedaubed
and forbidding faces, a sense of the peril which
hemmed us in came upon me. Should we ever again
pass that barrier of sinister faces ? I tried to tell
myself that we should, but it was not easy.

Wandering Spirit fixed me with the eyes that
always seemed to bore into one's very soul and
raising a hand as if to impress me with the importance of what he had to say, he began:

" You are one of them, the big Company. You
trade with the Crees for furs and write everything
down in a book. Tell me—you know: The Company sold this land to the Big Chief Woman; took
money for it. Why did they do that ? This land
belongs to us. The Company did not own it.
But they are rich because they got much money
for something that was not theirs. We are not rich.
We are poor. Often we do not have enough to
eat. So we have taken back the land, and when it
is sold again—to the Long-Knives (Americans)—
the money will come to us, not to the Company.

" You saw what happened the other day; how
Sioux Speaker and those other men dropped. It is
iyamun when the Crees make war ! Plenty blood
runs. This, that began the other day—it will go
on until there are no longer any Canadians here.
That was my vow when I fired the first shot. Now,
say: Why did they sell the land ? How much did
they get ? "

I realized the need for carefully-considered replies

to any questions he might put to me. I was in no
hurry to answer. Wandering Spirit, backed no
doubt by Imasees, had set a trap for me. I was the
only living white man who had witnessed the
butchery at Frog Lake. It gave him, I think, a
sense of uneasiness when he looked at me and
recalled that. It was an omen of bad luck. On the
morning of that day of blood he had intended I
should die with the others, planned to that end,
ordering me again and again to join and stay with
them. But some friendly Indian, on one pretext
or another, was sure a moment later to take me
aside, so that when the fatal moment arrived with
the firing of the first shot I was in the trading shop,
fitting Yellow Bear with a cap. Wandering Spirit
had never forgiven me, I knew, for being still
alive and I had no doubt his mind was made up,
notwithstanding his professions of good will, to
remedy the miscarriage of his designs and dispose
of me at the earliest opportunity. That might arise
at any instant with a hasty slip of my tongue.

Wandering Spirit knew no English and our
conversation was carried on in Cree.

" I do not carry all these things in my head,"
I said at length, " but I will try to tell you. The
Hudson's Bay Company did not sell the country;
as you say, it was not theirs to sell. But the Great
Mother thought they had some rights. They had
been here two hundred years. That is a long time.
If you had lived for two hundred years on a piece
of land you would be very bitter if somebody took
it away. The Queen made a treaty with the Indians
and the Hudson's Bay Company had to give up the
land—most of it. They could not be driven out

—or where would the Indians have traded their furs ?—and they had to live somewhere; they had to have land for their posts. Now, you ask why the Great Mother paid money to the Company. I will tell you. The Company had been good to the Indians, so the Great Mother when she sent her money chiefs to make the treaty paid the Company three hundred thousand pounds."

Wandering Spirit clapped his hands over his mouth in the Cree gesture of astonishment too colossal for expression in words. Then he swung suddenly upon me and said in his peculiarly penetrative tones :

" You knew about the fighting at Duck Lake— knew before the bad day here. If you Company men were friends of the Crees, you would have told the news. You told us nothing."

The fight, between Riel and the North-West Mounted Police, occurred on March 26th; we had learned of it five days later. Frog Lake followed on April 2nd. This was April 4th. We had not thought it wise to say anything to the Indians about the rising at Duck Lake.

I said : " I overheard something of your talk. You knew all about it—more than we did. I could not tell you anything."

" Well, we will see how much you know now," he persisted. " Tell me all about it—the half-breed war ; how it started, who were killed, how many soldiers, where they are. Speak with one tongue."

He had given me a formidable and disturbing task. " Mr. Simpson brought me a *musinagan* from Pitt. It tells about Duck Lake—the fighting. I will get the paper and read it to you." I rose, but he stopped me with a gesture.

" If you saw it, you know what it says. You don't need the paper."

My position had now reached a point of extreme difficulty and danger. I could not rely on memory to give him exact details of the battle or of the movements and numbers of troops—already on their way from the East to the Saskatchewan. Yet there were half-breeds in the camp able to read English and I knew that the paper would be taken and read by one of them following this examination and that any trifling discrepancy would be seized on by Wandering Spirit to fix upon me a charge of false-hood and attempt to mislead the band. A pretext to denounce me as an enemy of the Crees was all that was wanted by Wandering Spirit.

" You must think me very wise, Kahpaypamah-chakwayo," I replied. " I am not so clever. You do not make it easy for me; you make it hard." I looked round at the rows of tense, unsmiling faces. Some of them, I knew, were my friends.

" Hear—I am speaking to the council—I want to say, I will tell all I remember ! If I leave any-thing out that is in the paper—if I do not tell something exactly as it is there—do not say I spoke with two tongues. That will not be so ! " A shout of the approving " *How !* " ran round the circle. . I went on:

" The South Branch half-breeds, misled by Riel and other headmen, threatened to seize the traders' stores at Duck Lake. The chief of the mounted police, with fifty men, on the way from Fort Carlton to Duck Lake to protect the stores, met the half-breeds under Riel and Dumont and a battle followed. Eleven of the white men were killed;

some wounded. Some of the half-breeds and a few
of Beardy's Crees, also. A bullet ploughed through
Gabriel Dumont's scalp; the white chief was
wounded in the face. The police had returned to
Carlton. The head chief of the mounted police
had arrived there with one hundred more men,
but he had burned Fort Carlton and moved down
to Prince Albert. One of the Queen's big soldier
chiefs had reached the Touchwood Hills with two
thousand men. More soldiers were following from
Red River. An——"

" I don't believe all this ! " Wandering Spirit
broke in excitedly. " Liar ! "

I looked him in the eye. " You asked me to
tell you what the paper says. I am telling you.
I don't know whether it's true or not. Some things
I am not very sure about. But about the soldiers
—I remember that."

" You seem to remember everything against
us—all this talk of soldiers coming to fight us,"
he sneered. He regarded me darkly for a moment;
then: " I am going to ask another question. A
minute ago you wanted everyone to hear you.
Let them hear you now when you answer: Do you
want to see Riel win, or the whites ? Whose side
are you on ? "

I hope never again to find myself in so critical
a predicament. I could not bring myself, in no
matter what extremity, to say I sided with these
cut-throats, even though, because the thought of
death so appalled me just then, I had taken the
hand held out to me by the arch-assassin when he
promised on the demand of Oneepohayo that
I should not be harmed—that lean, claw-like hand

the closing of which half an hour before had loosed
the ball that stretched poor Quinn dead at his feet.

What I finally did say—and I spoke to the whole
council—was:

" The other day you made us—ten white men
—prisoners, over yonder. A little later nine died.
I am glad that I am alive—that you saved me—
but I have no life of my own any more. It is yours.
I am in your camp. Who can I side with ? "

I was manœuvring to avoid stating a deliberate
falsehood, but the effect to me was startling. I had
looked for quick manifestations of anger over an
evasive answer. What I met was a chorus of approval
of my reply. In brief, I had made a hit. But not
with Wandering Spirit. Of that his face was the
unspoken evidence.

I took advantage of a temporary lull in events
to move, with the air of regarding my position in
the camp as definitely established, to a seat in the
open space near Pritchard, about six feet in front
of Wandering Spirit. But a moment later he turned
on me again and said sharply:

" Say that you will stay with the Crees—will
help them, not try to get away ! "

I nodded.

I could see his eyes kindle as he looked off to
the right for a second; then he faced me again:
" Swear it ! " he commanded. " Raise your hand ! "

But the sympathy of many in the council had by this
swung over to me. They shouted " He did swear ! "

" *Namoya !* " retorted the war chief angrily.
" He did not ! "

A clamour of virulent dispute arose, my champions
asserting loudly that I had sworn, most of Big

Bear's men as vociferously combating the statement. The war of words mounted to an uproar,
till at length Wandering Spirit, fearing an actual
clash between the two factions, Wood and Plain
Crees, dropped the point and I escaped taking the
hateful oath.

I have many times thought over the occurrence
and long ago reached the conclusion that what
followed was just one detail, worked out probably
by Imasees or by Imasees and Wandering Spirit
together, in the game these two master-conspirators
had set out to play.

I question if, barring Big Bear himself and his
son-in-law, The Lone Man—perhaps the bravest
redskin I ever knew—there was in that whole camp
of two hundred lodges a single Indian who was
not afraid of Wandering Spirit. I do not except
even Imasees, truculent by nature though he was.
The Lone Man and the war chief hated each other
with a deadly enmity, but—because of that no
doubt—they also avoided one another, contact
spelling danger for both. No brave in his right
mind who wished to continue living would deliber-
ately have provoked Wandering Spirit.

Oseewoosgwan—Bald Head—was very old and
he had the mind of a very old man. That is why
I put him down a tool of Imasees. From his actions
and appearance I am certain no sense of danger
entered his shrunken old brain as, leaning heavily
on a stick, he pushed his way into the circle and
bending over, with a finger pointed derisively at
the war chief, piped in a high querulous falsetto:

" For what do you keep these white people here ?
You did not hold back the other day." He waved

a hand in the direction of the smoking desolation.
" But now you talk—just talk. You have done
bad already. It beats you to go on with what you
started, eh ? "

The blood surged to Wandering Spirit's face,
flushing it darkly, as he sat looking up from beneath
his war bonnet at the old man. Suddenly his right
hand shot out, throwing the lever of his Winchester
down in the action of loading and thereby raising
the muzzle.

He jumped to his feet. " You will see to-day
whether it beats me ! " he shouted.

But rapid as had been his movements, Louis
Patenaude and Alexis Crossarms had anticipated
them. They were both on their feet at his left;
in one hand Louis grasped the barrel of the Winchester and held it above his head; behind, Alexis
reinforced his hold with a double grip of his own
on the gun. Any effort by the now infuriated leader
to control the weapon was effectually blocked.
In vain he struggled to lower the barrel, to raise
the butt to his shoulder. Alexis and Louis held
the Winchester as in a vice.

I had leaped to my feet at the first move of the
war chief and now stood with muscles tensed,
oblivious to everything else, watching with fascin-
ated interest the drama being played out before me.
How would it end ? If the maddened war chief
succeeded by any chance in wresting the gun from
my defenders I was ready to throw myself upon
him and seize the rifle before he could level and
discharge it at me. At Frog Lake I had walked
along, while rifles cracked and screams and whoops
and war-cries a hundred yards away made a stunning

horror of the golden April morning, weaponless, like a man with hands bound, my eyes on the ground before me, expecting each instant a bullet in the back. Here at least there was certainty of action. I would go down, if it was my fate, fighting—I hoped with a kind of wild joy, bringing others down with me—not like a dog! I was too engrossed at the moment to feel any sense of fear.

A long knife stuck in a sheath in Wandering Spirit's belt. Both the war chief's hands were engaged with his gun. Patenaude bent forward suddenly and with his right hand plucked the knife from the sheath and raising his arm, held the point poised an inch above Wandering Spirit's heart. Then he craned forward until his face almost met that of the war chief and with eyes that glittered under the black brows like a snake's, bent upon the eyes opposing them a look of such calculated deadliness that in the hush that fell upon the staring council only the subdued clicking of stealthily-lifted gun-hammers could be heard.

The war chief's fury died under the menace of those level eyes, and over the copper features spread a film of dull grey, like dusted ashes. But he still fought, though without his former desperate reck-lessness, for possession of the Winchester.

Gladieu had risen with Wandering Spirit and his gun was now levelled on the war chief's head from behind. The hilt of the knife protruded above Louis' hand. Imasees, who had also risen and stood at Wandering Spirit's back, reached under his shoulder, grasped the protruding handle and with a sudden jerk drew the knife through, leaving an ugly gash across Louis' fingers. Then Imasees,

G

with outstretched arms and the naked blade in his left hand flashing in the sun, glanced quickly round the circle and spoke, in low, emotionless tones:

" This is not the way to do ! It will make trouble between us. We want to be all friends ! "

The way of retreat had been opened for Wandering Spirit. He seized it eagerly—no doubt gratefully.

" *Uh-huh* ! " he exclaimed, his head nodding to emphasize his agreement. " *Tapwa* ! (True !) The old man's talk made my heart bad, but that is past. We are all Crees here, all brothers ! "

Alexis and Louis had kept their hold on the rifle, but when Wandering Spirit lowered the hammer they released it. Gladieu stepped over, pushed his shoulder against that of the war chief and his rifle alongside the Winchester and watched narrowly while the two guns came down together. The significance of Gladieu's action lay in the fact that he distrusted the war chief's professed change of heart. He was guarding against a feint—a surprise by Wandering Spirit once control of his Winchester had passed again into his own hands.

Wandering Spirit was seated once more, but I still stood, absorbed as ever, awaiting the next development. He looked up presently and motioned with his hand.

" *Apee* ! " he said. " Sit ! *Numanando keeah* ! " For which there is no adequate translation. What he meant to convey was that I was not in danger at the moment. Which was satisfactory as far as it went.

The strain had proved too much for the war chief and as he sat before me I noted the violent shaking of his hands and knees, which he sought in vain to control. The depression that had come over him he was unable to throw off, and in a few minutes he had left the circle and the council was over.

Big Bear stopped me on my way back to Patenaude's lodge.

"Okemasis," said the chief, "you were foolish to stand up just now. Any could have shot you without danger to the others. Sitting you were safer."

I saw the force of Big Bear's statement. Pritchard said: "How did you ever get up? I could not have moved to save my life. They could have knocked me on the head like a rabbit."

Fitzpatrick had tried to rise, but Big Bear, who sat behind him, pulled him down. So the old chief not only preached common-sense; he put it into practice.

It was some time before the war chief made any further attempt to dispose of me and nothing I experienced later tried me as did the ordeal I had just successfully weathered.

I was walking through the camp a day or two later. The drummers were beating the big drum; the war song rose above the assembled braves. I glanced over at the group and gasped. Two warriors shuffled up and down in the war dance, over their shoulders the gilt and white vestments of their most unworldly and inoffensive victims, the dead priests. I was not a Roman Catholic, but apart from its, for me, poignant personal significance, the sight so completely outraged those feelings of reverence I had been brought up to entertain for all things sacred that I could only stand and stare. It remains among my most vivid impressions of that terrible two months.

CHAPTER XI

For the first few days after the massacre the Indians gave themselves up largely to feasting and dancing. Some four hundred head of work cattle and milk cows, supplied to the Wood Crees in the district, were rounded up and herded near the camp. Besides the provisions and other goods obtained from the two posts, they had looted the dwellings of the missionaries, government officials and settlers at Frog Lake and in the surrounding territory. Every day for the first few weeks eight or ten head . of cattle were shot, and besides beef there was flour, tea, sugar, bacon and tobacco in plenty. The Indian revelled in the unaccustomed abundance and it is not to be wondered at that he grew wasteful. To the prisoners, on the other hand, these were days of supreme wretchedness and anxiety.

The oxen had been supplied to the various bands for agricultural purposes and the cows were intended to form the nucleus of a herd which it was the plan of the government to distribute among the Indians as they became sufficiently trustworthy properly to care for them. The animals before the outbreak had been in the keeping of some of the more progressive men of the three Wood Cree bands at Frog Lake. These Indians still asserted a personal property in the cattle and soon bad blood began to show itself between them and Big Bear's men, who refused to recognize any individual interests in the herd and slew the animals as their whims and appetites dictated.

The two hundred lodges composing the camp were pitched in an oblong circle enclosing a considerable space. One evening about sundown while strolling through the camp I noticed two Indians, one armed, the other not, disputing hotly a short way in front of me. Suddenly the man with the gun clubbed it and brought it down in a vicious swing on the other's head, laying him flat. He then walked off.

In a few minutes the other got up, howling with rage and pain, blood streaming down his face, and staggered to his lodge. He reappeared immediately with a gun and, still howling, started in the direction of the Plain Cree lodges at the upper end of the camp. Two of his friends stole up behind him, seized his arms and took away his weapon. Had he reached the other man's lodge he would of course have been killed. In a second encounter his assailant would not have hesitated to substitute the load in his gun for the barrel. I afterward learned that they had quarrelled over some cattle claimed by the Wood Cree.

There was danger and excitement in the camp when the cattle were slaughtered each day. It brought back to the Indians old times and the buffalo hunt. They ran the cattle on horseback and shot them and were not always careful about the direction of their bullets. If a steer dodged among the lodges the man on horseback followed and fired at the first opportunity. Sometimes the bullet hit the steer; sometimes it went through a lodge—to the consternation of the inmates.

I walked over occasionally to see them dispose of a kill. As soon as it fell it was bled. Then it was turned on its back and skinned down either side, the hide being spread out to cover as much ground as possible and serve as a table on which to lay out the meat. Squaws and children, interested spectators, crowded about the carcase. The butcher parcelled out the animal, handed a piece to each and they went away happy. In the earlier part of my captivity I never wanted for beef.

One bright afternoon, three or four days after the massacre, I was lying in Patenaude's lodge when I heard Big Bear speaking. The Indians had danced and orated daily since the outbreak, but I had kept away from them, knowing that their talk was only of violence and bloodshed. When I heard the old chief, however, my curiosity was excited. He had seemed depressed ever since the rising; he had avoided these dances of Wandering Spirit and the young men and so far as I knew had not yet publicly spoken his mind to his band on the outrages. I was anxious to hear what he had to say.

The warriors to the number of sixty were seated in the form of a horseshoe on the ground at the upper end of the camp. Big Bear occupied the centre. At the top sat Wandering Spirit with the other councillors and I stretched myself at the open end opposite them where I could observe the war chief, towards whom my eyes were irresistibly drawn whenever he was in sight. Big Bear spoke in Cree and I caught only the close of his speech. He said:

" *Kias* I was a chief. Long ago, when we fought

the Blackfeet, not a man among you could do what
I did. All the South Nations—the Bloods, Peigans,
Blackfeet, Crows, Sioux—knew Big Bear; that he
was head chief of all the Crees. At that time if
I said anything you listened to me—you obeyed
me. But now I say *one* thing and *you* do another ! ''

He bent over and swept his arm in the faces of
Wandering Spirit and the other councillors, who
sat with lowered eyes, and pointed in the direction
of the smouldering ruins of Frog Lake. The old
man stood for a moment in this dramatic pose,
his face quivering with emotion; then he folded
his soiled grey blanket about him with an air of
impressive dignity and strode away, a pathetic
but still commanding figure. He entered Mr.
Simpson's tent and I followed. He had noticed
me as he walked off and looking up as I came in
said, with a wave of his hand:

" I have got the name of being a bad man, but
Missa Jim here, my oldest friend, can tell you
that is not true. In the old days, when the Company
sold rum and I drank it, I did not get ugly and
wish to make trouble like the others. To sit quietly
and sing—that was what I liked, as Missa Jim
knows. I have always been the friend of the white
man. I am sorry for what was done. I am more
than sorry for my brother, Delaney. Had I only
been near when the shooting began, I should have
saved him, at least.''

The Indians were preparing to go down and
attack Fort Pitt. Mr. Simpson and I thought this
a good opportunity to suggest to Big Bear that the
police under Inspector Dickens and the handful
of settlers who had fled to the fort for refuge, be

allowed to leave Pitt unmolested, in consideration of their abandoning the place without a fight. Pitt was a fort in name only—in reality, a group of unprotected wooden buildings—and we knew that it would be impossible for the little garrison of thirty men to hold out for any length of time against the three hundred armed hostiles. Big Bear readily agreed to call a council and urge upon his band the adoption of our advice, before they left for Pitt.

CHAPTER XII

A COUNCIL OF WAR

A WEEK later the camp-crier one morning went up and down among the lodges to call the warriors, and Simpson, Fitzpatrick, Halpin—who had arrived from Cold Lake—and myself, to a council. They were going, he said, to Fort Pitt on the following morning to take it and wanted to talk over and decide on the best plans for accomplishing their object before they left.

We found the old chief and his men forming a large double circle in the dancing tent, a big lodge formed of several smaller ones. Big Bear sat in state at one side within the circle. Beside him on the right sat Wandering Spirit, wearing his war bonnet with the five glistening eagle plumes. He was filling an old stone pipe belonging to the chief with tobacco and red willow bark.

Big Bear was in an amiable mood. He grew reminiscent as the pipe was handed to him.

" This pipe is very dear to me," he said. " It was smoked by all my wives in turn. One by one they have gone to the Sand Hills, and this is all I have to remember them by."

Followed the ceremony of lighting the Peace Pipe in council. Taking the stem between his lips, Big Bear applied the lighted match handed to him by Wandering Spirit to the bowl. He took a long pull and tightly closing his lips so that none of the smoke should escape, turned the stem in succession to the four cardinal points of the compass, then toward the ground; finally, bowing his head, he raised it straight up before him, so that the Great Spirit might be first to smoke. After this he blew the first draught of smoke from his own lips, muttered a prayer and after taking a few draws himself, passed the pipe to the man on his left. It then travelled from mouth to mouth, each warrior in turn taking a few pulls, around the circle. The purpose of this ceremony is to propitiate the Kitse Manito and ask his guidance in the matter before the council. It will be noticed that the pipe follows the course of the sun, indicating the association of his deity in the mind of the red man with the most powerful visible celestial body in his simple and beautiful religion.

When all, ourselves included, had smoked, Big Bear rose and spoke, making a strong plea for the course urged upon him by Simpson and myself and asking those present to state their views, we white men first as having a knowledge of the usages of our nations in war. Fitzpatrick—an American ex-soldier—Simpson and myself, in turn, begged the warriors to be guided by their chief, assuring them they would never regret sparing the lives of the comparatively defenceless people at Pitt, among them many women and children. It was customary, we said, for a superior force to allow a small body of the enemy to surrender and march off unharmed, rather than to attack them.

Several Indians followed and supported our plan. One man thanked us for the suggestion. It would be much simpler to lure the police out of the fort by fair promises and then surround and kill them in the open than to attack them under cover of the buildings. Wandering Spirit said they had not spared our lives thus far to have us dictate to them what they should do in time of war. Imasees said Riel's orders were to kill the police. As for the Plain Crees, they meant to fight. They had men enough to capture and burn the fort and kill everyone in it. If the police went they would take with them their guns and ammunition, things the Indians most needed.

The council broke up and we went back to our tents, saddened and discouraged. Our efforts had come to nothing, apparently. There was slight chance the suggestions we had made would serve any purpose, except to further a plot to wipe out the garrison at Pitt by treachery instead of in open attack. Big Bear, however, promised if possible to get the police away in safety and the sequel shows that the old chief was not unmindful of his word.

Early next morning the crier again went through the camp. The warriors were to prepare to go to Pitt. Missa Jim and his young men (Halpin and myself) must accompany them. Simpson and I were sitting in his tent when these commands reached our ears.

" The swine ! " exploded the old man. " They want to use us—make us write letters to decoy the police out of the fort, so that they can kill them like sheep. I'll see them damned first ! They won't get me to go."

" Or me," I said. " Life is sweet, but I don't value mine as against those of thirty of my fellows."

Simpson called his stepsons, Louis and Benjamin Patenaude, and they came with their guns. A moment

later Wandering Spirit, with Imasees and two of
the murderers, entered. The war chief expressed
surprise that we were not preparing to go to Pitt.
He ordered us to get ready at once.

Then Louis Patenaude got up—and there was
in his black eyes that deadly gleam that I—and
the war chief—had seen in them when he held the
knife over Wandering Spirit's heart.

/" My stepfather," he said, " is not strong. He
is an old man. He has lived among you since he
was a boy and has always used you well. But how
have you used him ? Why are you persecuting him ?
You have taken his horses, you have looted and
burned his house. Isn't that enough, that you should
wish to drag him after you around the country ?
He will not go ! "

The four were armed and painted, but the war
chief did not care again to provoke Louis.

" But the young man ? " he said, indicating me.

" Tell him I'm staying with Mr. Simpson,"
I said. " He is my chief and my place is with him."

The war chief submitted, but his anger was
evident. They got up and went out. As Imasees
reached the door, he turned and said over his
shoulder :

/" Remember, if any of our people are hurt at Pitt,
it will be hard to keep the young men from doing
harm when they get back."

It was his parting shot. For our refusal to assist
in their treacherous scheme, we were to be held
accountable should any of them suffer. Under
these circumstances, it may be imagined that our
feelings were not the cheerfulest during the next
few days.

Only a few old men, women and children were
left at Frog Lake. The warriors, mounted, assembled
at the lower end of the camp. They, as well as
their ponies, were decked in all their finery. With
their paint and feathers, their polished weapons,
gaudy blankets, beaded leggings and moccasins,
they made a picturesque panorama against the
setting of green grass and delicate aspens, the
distant hills, the glint of blue waters in the lakes
below, and immediately behind, the white-canvas
lodges with their smoke-browned tops and crossed
poles. They came riding slowly around the camp,
their war-chant rising weirdly on the fresh spring
air, their ponies prancing under their flashy trap-
pings. They reached the far end again, broke into
a gallop and with wild cries and a crash from their
guns, clattered away in the direction of Fort Pitt.

Halpin was the only white man to accompany
them; he had no option. Simpson, Fitzpatrick and
myself might easily have escaped in their absence,
but there were the two white women in the camp;
we might yet be able to do them some service.
At all events they could not but have felt that we
had deserted them had they been left alone among
these savages and we could not have found it in
our hearts to go. In any case, almost all the bands
for three hundred miles east along both Saskatchewans we knew had risen and the whites in the country
had taken refuge in the police forts and towns
which had been fortified; the prospect of being
able to bring relief to the other prisoners could we
have reached Battleford in safety was slight, and
Battleford, the nearest fort or settlement, was more
than a hundred miles away, surrounded by hostiles

who had murdered and pillaged just as had those in whose hands we were. Moreover, Big Bear's band had asserted that should one escape they would kill all other prisoners. This threat alone was sufficient to hold us.

So we sat down to wait with what patience we might for the return of the belligerents from Fort Pitt.

Henry Quinn arrived on the morning of April 3rd at Fort Pitt, after his thirty-five mile tramp through the slush under the friendly cover of a moonless night. Warned by Mondion, he had managed to slip away unobserved from Frog Lake through the thicketed hollows shortly before the massacre began. In fact he had gone only a mile or two and after crossing a chain of low-lying lakes, was working his way stealthily up through the hills on the other side, when the faint mutter of rifle-fire reached his ear, mounted and died away. Quinn was a nephew of the murdered Indian agent. He had no difficulty in accounting for these sounds or in interpreting to Captain Dickens what had occurred at the settlement—information confirming reports brought to Pitt by George Mann, farming instructor at Onion Lake, who had arrived there with his family the previous night. Mann had been told of the massacre by friendly Indian runners who had witnessed it. Quinn was sworn in by Captain Dickens as a special constable.

TOM QUINN.   CAPT. DICKENS.   JAMES K. SIMPSON.   STANLEY SIMPSON.   ANGUS McKAY.

GROUP AT FORT PITT, 1884.

Facing p. 110.

CHAPTER XIII

THE FALL OF FORT PITT

On the morning of April 14th, Corporal Cowan, Constable Loasby and Henry Quinn left Fort Pitt on a scouting trip. A little later Big Bear's warriors appeared at the top of the hill, 800 yards behind the fort, demanding its surrender and that the police give up their arms. Little Poplar, who was camped with his family on the south bank of the Saskatchewan opposite Pitt, first saw the hostiles and with characteristic Indian inconsistency warned the garrison.

To this demand Captain Dickens replied that he would hold the fort while there was a man able to point a gun. The Indians held a council and decided that its capture by direct attack would cost them too many men. They therefore sent a second message to say that the police would be allowed to evacuate the fort without molestation if they would do so. Big Bear and Little Poplar accomplished this. The old chief's letter, written by Halpin, reads as follows:

" Fort Pitt,
" April 14th, 1885.

" Sergeant Martin, N.W.M.P.

" My dear Friend,

" Since I first met you long ago, we have always been good friends. That is the reason why I want to speak kindly to you : please get off from Fort Pitt as soon as you can. Tell your Captain that I remember him well, for since the Canadian government has had me to starve in this country he sometimes gave me food. I do not forget, the last time I visited Pitt he gave me a good blanket. That is the reason that I want you all out without any bloodshed. We had a talk, I and my men, before we left camp at Frog Lake and thought the way we are doing now the best, that is to let you off if you would go. Try and get away before the afternoon, as the young men are all wild and hard to keep in hand.

"BIG BEAR.

" P.S.

" You asked me to keep the men in camp last night and I did, so I want you to get off to-day.

"BIG BEAR."

Captain Dickens still refused to move and the Indians next day resorted to strategy. They invited W. J. McLean, chief trader of the Hudson's Bay Company in charge at Pitt, to a parley in the open ground half-way between the fort and the camp. Against the advice of Captain Dickens, McLean went, taking with him as interpreter a half-breed, François Dufresne. Without exciting his suspicions, they gradually drew McLean away until out of range of the fort and then told him the discussion would be concluded in their camp. McLean had no alternative but to go with them. They were all seated, McLean urging them to return to Frog Lake and abandon the idea of taking Pitt, when the three scouts, Cowan, Loasby and Quinn, returning from their trip, came suddenly in view and attempted to ride past the camp.

Instantly all was excitement The Indians seized their guns and rushed to cut off the scouts. It was over in a few moments—the garrison at the fort took a hand—but the account of this must be reserved for another chapter.

Alarmed by the firing, McLean jumped to his

feet and said he must return to the fort. Wandering Spirit levelled his rifle on him, but Little Poplar threw his arms around McLean. The war chief placed his hand on the chief trader's shoulder.

" You stay here ! " he stated bluntly. " You are a prisoner."

At the command of the Indians, Mr. McLean then wrote the following letter :

> " TOP OF THE HILL, FORT PITT,
> " *April 15th*, 2 *p.m.*

" MY DEAR WIFE,

" Most unfortunately I have been too confiding in the Indians and have come into camp. After I had had a long talk with them and they had spoken at length, they would not have it otherwise than that the police must and should go away at once. I continued talking with a view of gaining time for the three men who were out. They, the scouts, came on the main road and firing ensued. Immediately the whole camp went after them. I thought the Indians were aware of the men being out and said nothing about them. Had I spoken, perhaps things might have been different. Now, in the excitement, they have made me prisoner and have made me swear by Almighty God that I will stay with them.

" Alas, that I came into the camp at all, for God only knows how things will turn out now. They want you and the children to come into camp and it may be for the best that you should. If the police cannot get off the Indians are sure to attack to-night, they say, and will burn the fort. I am really at a loss what to suggest for the best. For the time being we might be safe with the Indians, but provisions will be scarce after a short time and we may suffer. The chiefs and councillors say they will let me go down the Beaver River with my family, and if so we should be all right. Stanley must come also and everyone connected with the Company. They want Malcolm and Hodson also. I will write you again after hearing what Captain Dickens says about allowing you all to come out. I candidly

H

believe it best that you should come, as the Indians
are determined to burn the fort if the police do not leave.
They have brought coal oil with them for the purpose
and I fear they will succeed in setting fire to the place.
The Indians promise that beyond a doubt after you
all come out they will retire and give the police time
to get off before making any move. They wish you to
bring your things at once. We must do all we can to
move out before dark so as to give Captain Dickens and
his men a chance to get away. May God bless and guide
you all for the best.

"W. J. McLean."

On receipt of this letter Mr. McLean's family,
the civilians and the Company's servants prepared
to join him.

The position of the police was now most pre-
carious and a retreat was ordered. There was no
longer any reason why Dickens should attempt to
hold Pitt, since he and his men alone remained.
But little time was left for preparation. Ammunition
and provisions were placed in the scow and carrying
the wounded scout, Loasby, with them, the detachment marched down to the landing. The scow
was launched, but water poured in through the
open seams. It seemed for a time as if it would
be impossible to cross the river. There was an
interval of dreadful suspense—that the Indians
would take advantage of the delay and attack was
anticipated by everybody. But Big Bear kept his
word and with the help of Little Poplar held in
check the more truculent members of his band.
At last the opposite shore was reached. Little
Poplar's family was in camp there and the part of
the sub-chief in restraining the young men loses
some of its glamour from this fact.

It was a terrible night. A terrific storm raged,

the river had broken only on the 10th and great blocks of ice raced on its turgid angry flood—but let me quote from the diary of Corporal R. B. Sleigh, the gallant soldier who had left Frog Lake just before the outbreak and escaped so many dangers, only to meet kismet a little later:

April 2—Constable Roby left with team for Onion Lake, brought back lumber. Indians out there terribly excited. Mr. Mann, farm instructor, with wife and family arrived at 1 a.m. with report all whites killed at Frog Lake. Assembly at 12 p.m. All hands working all night, blocking windows and making loopholes in all buildings. Double picket.

3— Good Friday. Henry Quinn in from Frog Lake, reported all whites shot. They were led out for execution, when he ran for his life and managed to escape ; poor fellow played out and showed good grit. Everybody busy pulling down outside buildings and barricading fort.

5— Mr. Quinney, Episcopal clergyman escaped from Onion Lake, held short service. Indians heard shouting on hill during night ; shots fired.

7—Stockade being erected. The Misses McLean show great courage and each, rifle in hand, stands at a loophole. Men work like horses and are cheerful. All civilians sworn in and armed. Bastion put up left front of fort. Sentries in each house ; four hours duty each. 9—Second bastion put up orderly-room corner.

14—No relief ; things look blue. Everybody in good spirits. Body of Indians at top of hill ; 800 yards from fort ; 250 Indians armed and mounted. Big Bear sent letter down ; everybody to evacuate fort and give up arms. Doors barricaded ; men in places. Big war dance on hill. Indians skulking through woods in every direction. Double sentries on barracks.

15—Hudson's Bay Company employees, 28 in number, gave themselves up to Big Bear. Impossible to hold fort now, so had to retire gracefully, carrying Loasby, across the river in scow and camp for the night, not forgetting to bring colours along. Nearly swamped in crossing; scow leaking badly. General idea prevailed we would be attacked going down river. Thus ended the siege of Fort Pitt.

16—Up at 4.30 after a wretched night; snowing fast and very windy. Moving slow. Several men frost-bitten. Clothing frozen on our backs. 17—Started 7 a.m. Ice running very strong. Some narrow escapes in ice jams. Camped at 9 for dinner. Resumed trip at noon. 18—Dull and cold. Much ice running. 19—Left Slapjack Island 7.13 a.m. Ran five hours. Camped Beaver Island. Ran three hours; camped Pine Island for night. 20—Here all day. Barricaded scow; inspected arms. Rough-looking parade. Wounded man better. 21—Left 7 a.m. At 11 hailed Josie Alexander and two policemen on south bank with despatches for us. Battleford safe; troops expected daily. Ran all day; stopped small island for night. River falling; stuck on sandbars. All slept aboard scow; two men on picket.

22—Started 5.45 a.m., reached Battleford 9 a.m. Garrison turned out and presented arms. Police band played us into fort. Enthusiastic greeting. Ladies gave us a grand dinner.

Among the valuable things secured by the Indians at Pitt, was the gold watch worn by Charles Dickens and bequeathed by him at his death to his son, Captain Francis J. Dickens. The police were obliged to leave practically all their personal property when they quit Fort Pitt and in his anxiety for the safety of his men the captain must have forgotten for the moment that his famous father's most cherished gift to him, this watch, was in his trunk. A few days later a half-breed, Alfred Schmidt, showed me the watch at Frog Lake.

" I give you for fifteen dollar," he said.

I examined it closely. The engraving on the outside of the case had been partially effaced by wear. On the inside was traced the name " Charles Dickens " and a date. A small gold locket attached to the chain held a miniature of his wife and a braid of her hair.

I should have liked to secure the watch, with the view of returning it to the captain should our paths ever cross again. This seemed so problematical as to make it appear hardly worth while planning for the future. Besides, the Indians had appropriated everything I possessed, including my money; fifteen dollars was away beyond my depth. However, I had the satisfaction of learning from the captain later at Battleford that he had recovered his prized memento on the surrender of the hostiles and as he died the following summer in Indianapolis, the well-worn timepiece which served to mark the hours devoted to the fortunes of David Copperfield and the delightful excursions and mishaps of the ingenuous Mr. Pickwick, and at which we can imagine the great author so often glancing, is now no doubt in the possession of one of his other sons or daughters.

Louis Patenaude gave me an amusing account of the looting of Fort Pitt.

Forcing the doors of the H. B. stores, the Indians rushed in. Each seized the first thing he could put his hands on. It might be a cask of sugar, a chest of tea, a princely fur, a bolt of calico, a caddy of tobacco, a keg of nails—it was all one. Off he rushed, set it down outside and hurried back for more. When he returned his first prize was certain to be gone; another—a weaker brother—had appropriated it. A woman might get hold of a fine wool shawl, some buck fancy it for his wife and she would be forcibly dispossessed. It was bedlam and war for the spoils, Indian expletives mingling with blows and outcries. Tins of Crosse & Black-well's Yarmouth Bloaters, jars of pickled walnuts and pâté de foie gras, imported at great expense all the way from London, were slashed open with knives, sniffed at and flung on the ground. The police hospital stores were got at. The red men evidently believed all medicines in use by the police were " comforts " ; they drank them, until one old man nearly succumbed; then they decided the enemy had tried to poison them. They hesitated to use the sacks of flour piled in tiers for the defence of the fort; the police, they thought, might have mixed strychnine with it.

Between the suspense and the blizzard that raged, the night of April 15th, 1885, to me in the Indian camp at Frog Lake was one of the most miserable I have ever experienced. The Indians had taken the blankets off my own bed at the time of the outbreak and had not Patenaude secured for me somehow a tanned cowhide with the hair remaining I should have had nothing to cover me when I slept. On this night the snow sifted down through the poles at the open top of the lodge and wet me through as I lay on the damp hard ground. I shivered with the cold and could sleep only in fitful snatches.

Next day was bright and warm, but two feet of snow had piled up during the night. That evening shortly after dark a messenger arrived with news of the bloodless victory of the Indians at Pitt. His horse had waded through snow to his belly and was steaming with sweat. It may be imagined with what relief this information was received by us, for the threat of Imasees was still fresh in our

minds. By the Indian code, blood demands blood.
If a fellow-tribesman is slain by an enemy, any
other member of the nation to which the slayer
belongs may pay with his life. The red man's
vengeance is no respecter of persons.

The day following, all the band came in with
their captives. We now had other prisoners to
share our troubles and we felt better. The new
arrivals included three young ladies, the daughters
of Mr. McLean. Misery always did love company.

The prisoners in the camp after the fall of Pitt
were, besides Mr. McLean and his family, James
K. Simpson, F. Stanley Simpson, John Fitzpatrick,
Rev. Père Legoff, Mrs. Gowanlock, Mrs. Delaney,
Rev. Chas. Quinney and wife, George G. Mann
and family, H. R. Halpin, J. B. Poirier, Malcolm
McDonald, Robert Hodson, Otto and François
Dufresne, Henry Quinn, John Pritchard and myself.
There were besides a number of half-breeds, osten-
sibly prisoners, but some of whom at least I should
be slow to list in that category.

CHAPTER XIV

THREE SCOUTS

LET me now return and follow the fortunes of the three scouts, Cowan, Loasby and Quinn, who left Fort Pitt shortly before Big Bear and his men appeared on the hill behind it the morning of April 14th.

The trail from Fort Pitt to Frog Lake is a fairly good one in summer, but the scouts did not follow it. They went out along the river, which runs a few miles to the south. They travelled slowly, reconnoitring the ground ahead from commanding rises, and not until sunrise next morning were they looking through their glasses from the wooded slopes across the chain of lakes at the site of the Frog Lake settlement and the two hundred lodges a short way beyond.

They observed a number of things. First, that where the settlement had been there was no longer anything but a collection of charred and deserted ruins. Again, that the camp was still where Quinn had last seen it ; at least the lodges. The most important thing of all they also noted, but unfortunately its significance did not then strike them. This was the fact that very little life was observable about the camp. Why, the little scouting detail was to discover later to its cost.

When Corporal Cowan and his companions left Frog Lake on their return to Pitt—I give the story as Quinn told it to me—they again avoided the trail. The Indian camp was behind them, true, but there might be hostile parties prowling about the country and the white men had no desire to run into a band that would likely greatly outnumber them. As they drew near Fort Pitt, however, without having sighted an enemy, they put aside a caution they now considered unnecessary and struck over to the trail. Quinn always maintained this was contrary to his advice, but Cowan was in command.

They had not followed it far until they saw that the trail was marked with many hoof-prints. Quinn dismounted and examined it closely.

" I'm right, Cowan ! " he exclaimed, looking up. " I said the Indians were ahead of us. Well, they are. They've come down the trail as we went out along the river. Here's the track of a shod horse —my uncle's mare that Wandering Spirit took the day of the massacre. I put those shoes on myself. I know them."

Cowan disagreed. " The police have been out during the day, rounding up the stock. That accounts for the tracks. The whole camp was at Frog Lake still, wasn't it ? "

" The camp, yes—the lodges, but remember we saw mighty few Indians," Quinn returned.

" Well, I'm not scared," said Cowan. " We're going on, anyhow. Funk, that's what's wrong with you, Quinn."

To which Quinn retorted angrily that he could go anywhere Cowan dared. They rode on in silence.

But as it happened, Quinn was right, Cowan wrong.

Fort Pitt was now little more than a mile away and just over the crest of the slope behind it, out of sight of the fort, four hundred blood-drunken and painted savages were discussing energetically plans for getting the police outside the walls of the fort so that they might shoot them down with no risk to themselves.

The camp lay just to the left of the trail. Behind it a fringe of willows marked the course of a creek, and a break in this fringe at one point showed where the trail crossed the creek over a bridge.

When the three scouts looked from the bridge through the opening and saw the hostile camp ahead and to their left, they realized that they had made a mistake in quitting the river for the trail. But it was now too late to rectify it. Putting spurs to their horses, they dashed for the top of the slope.

The Indians saw them. Grabbing their guns, with wild cries of " *Chemoginusuk ! Chemoginusuk ! (Soldiers !   Soldiers !)*" they rushed for the trail to head them off.

Along its crest to the right of the trail, the slope was thickly wooded, shutting off any chance of getting through to the fort in that direction. They had no option but to stick to the trail.

It has been said that a man does not die until his time comes, and the tragedy of that wild ride through the Indian camp rests in the fact that the three men had come unscathed through that hail of lead and then, with safety just ahead, Cowan's horse, crazed no doubt by the excitement, stopped suddenly and—bucked !

In vain Cowan spurred him—he would not budge. Cowan dropped to the ground and ran. An Indian, his gun levelled on the policeman, raced alongside. Cowan put out a hand.

" Don't shoot, my brother ! " he said in Cree, and the redskin turned and left him.

But a puff of smoke came from the wood on the right and, with a bullet through his heart, poor Cowan pitched his length along the dusty trail.

Henry Quinn's escape down the hill by way of the trail had been cut off, and answering the fusillade of which he was the target with repeated shots from his own rifle—fortunately for himself later without doing any damage—he swung at top speed off to the right along the wooded slope and disappeared among the poplar bluffs up the river. The hostiles were too intent upon the capture of Fort Pitt to go after him.

Meanwhile Loasby was pounding down the slope in full view of the fort and safety as fast as his jaded mount would bear him. Lone Man—cool, crafty, daring, a human hawk whose clear brain never permitted his nerve or confidence to desert him—with flapping pinion of soiled white blanket, on the white racer that had unaccountably disappeared from his owner's stable one dark night a year before in Montana, followed swiftly after him.

A shot. The saddle seemed suddenly to have grown hot under Loasby. Blood trickled down his leg, but he rode on. Another shot. His horse stopped, swayed, a bullet in his neck.

Lone Man was close behind—too close. The chest of the white racer hit like a hammer on the rump of the policeman's stricken mount and down they went, over and over, the dying animal and the living, falcon redskin and wounded trooper.

Loasby was first on his feet. Half stunned, he did not stop to look round but ran.

Lone Man raised himself on one knee and at the crack of his rifle, Loasby tumbled with his face in the dust and the trail of a bullet through his body close to the spine.

And now the burst of fire which, since Loasby was apparently past the possibility of injury from it, there was no longer need to hold, came at the intrepid savage from the fort. But he writhed forward, on his belly like a snake, till he reached the policeman. He turned him over.

" I thought he was dead," Lone Man told me later, " or I would have finished him. But he ought to have killed me—he was first up."

Drawing his knife, he cut the belt, with its cartridges and revolver, circling Loasby's waist. Then he writhed back with it, gripping the grass with his crimsoned fingers, to his horse and galloped away up the slope. And all the while the bullets from the fort plugged viciously into the sod around him.

Loasby got on his feet again. He staggered to the gate in the fort, flung out derisive fingers in the direction of Lone Man and collapsed in the arms of the two men come to meet him. They carried him into the fort.

Henry Quinn halted in a grove of poplars a mile up the river from the fort, dismounted and tied his horse to a tree. Night fell, and under cover of the river-bank he crept cautiously down to the road leading from the fort to the stream. He could not approach the stockade in the darkness; the sentries would be nervous. Or a prowling redskin might write *finis* for him.

He drew his knife and dug and dug in the clay

bank. The cold gripped him; he shook violently. He must have shelter from the blinding storm! At length he had a hole, big enough to shield his body from the swirling snow, the ferocious wind. He crawled in. If only he had something—a crust, even! He was ravenous.

The hours dragged. At dawn he stood outside the stockade, calling for Sergeant Martin.

The curling black head of Wandering Spirit appeared suddenly at an upper window of one of the buildings. Fort Pitt was in the hands of the Indians!

Again there was a cry of " *Chemoginusuk!* " and a moment later Wandering Spirit was following a fresh footprint through the newly-fallen snow. It led to the river; there ended abruptly. The war chief stood on the bank, studying the mystery of the vanishing track. Where could he have gone, this policeman? The riddle was unsolvable, and presently he walked on along the bank, rifle in hand, searching every angle of the surroundings with his hawk-like eyes.

Another Indian—Isadore Mondion—followed the footprint from the fort to the river and stopped. Just beneath him a pair of legs stuck out of the bank. With one hand he motioned to the war chief; with the other he pointed downward. Wandering Spirit started toward him, running.

" Henry," said Mondion, " come out."

The poor scout, hiding like an ostrich, trembled but he did not move.

" Come out!" Mondion repeated sternly. " Quick, before Wandering Spirit comes! I will protect you."

Quinn crawled from his hole. The war chief, his rifle held threateningly before him hurried up. Mondion put a hand on Quinn ; he stepped in front of him.

"My prisoner, Kahpaypamahchakwayo ! " he said, meeting the war chief's lowering glance with one equally truculent. "*Payatik !* Be careful ! His life is mine—I give it to him. From to-day we are brothers, Henry and I."

The war chief's answer, Quinn thought, would never come. But at length, with a wave of his hand, "So be it, *neestas*," he replied. "But the life you give him—if he loves it, he will know better than to work against us ! He was with the police. And his rifle—that must be mine."

The rifle was surrendered and Mondion, his arm about his adopted brother, walked with him into the fort.

The warriors crowded round Quinn.

"His medicine is strong ! " they cried. "*Mistahay muskowow !* Bullets will not pierce him—three times he has escaped ! "

"*How ! How !* " shouted the camp. And Quinn was safe.

CHAPTER XV

PERILOUS MOMENTS

THE new prisoners were distributed among various members of the different Indian bands. My friend Stanley Simpson was taken in charge by Lone Man, the intrepid savage who had ridden down and shot Loasby.

A day or two after he arrived in camp, Simpson called on me one afternoon. He stayed until dark; then, being a stranger in the camp he did not fancy returning alone to Lone Man's lodge and I accompanied him. I sat for a few minutes talking with Lone Man before starting to return to Patenaude's lodge.

The trail led through the camp. I had no sooner emerged than I saw in the vague light cast over the camp by the lodge fires a profile I could not mistake. It was the head of Wandering Spirit, framed in its dark setting of curly hair—the profile of the one man I frankly dreaded in that camp of dreadful men and the sight of whom always set a faster pace for my heart. He had seen me go through the camp with Simpson and had stolen out to intercept me on my road back.

He bent forward beside the trail, his arms folded on his chest and his head inclined in my direction. The muzzle of his rifle protruded above the blanket drawn round his shoulders. It was the first time I had met him alone and at night since the massacre, and with my heart beating rapidly, though outwardly calm, I walked down the trail toward him. He halted me.

" Where have you been ? " he asked. I explained. What did Simpson and McLean think about the rising, he wanted to know ? I had not heard them say, I equivocated; did they really themselves know ? I doubted it. I brushed past him—walked on to Patenaude's lodge. I did not look behind, but queer ripples were chasing up and down my spine as I went along. Even now, as I write, I fall to wondering why he never took advantage of the frequent opportunities and finished me, as I never doubted he wished to do.

A week later five Cree runners from Poundmaker's reservation, near Battleford, arrived with messages from Riel. The half-breed rebel chief complimented Big Bear for his help at Frog Lake, asked him to effect a junction with Poundmaker and then attack and capture Battleford.

The stories told by the runners differed somewhat in detail. They had brought no direct message from Poundmaker and Big Bear's band apparently distrusted them. A council was called. The messengers were shown to the open space in its centre. The white men were summoned to attend and with the half-breeds they formed a segment of the circle.

Imasees was first to speak. He adjured the messengers, as they valued their lives, to tell the truth, the whole truth ; referring to their conflicting stories. Dressy Man argued that they should be received as friends, without suspicion.

Wandering Spirit, seated apart from the others at the lower end of the circle, listened with ill-disguised impatience to Dressy Man's pacific harangue. His rifle rested against his shoulder and he stabbed viciously in the sod before him with the long hunting-knife in his left hand. As usual my gaze was drawn to him, and, as he glanced up frequently and our eyes met, a black scowl settled upon his face.

As Dressy Man finished, the war chief sprang to his feet. He threw doubt on the professions of the messengers. Who knew but that they were emissaries of the whites and wished to lead the band into a trap? Why had no message come from Poundmaker? For his part, he preferred to go to Duck Lake direct and join Riel.

"There's another thing I want to talk about," he went on, his soft voice rising into its ominous ring—and here the real purport of his speech revealed itself: "When I began this war, over there "—he raised an arm and pointed in the direction of Frog Lake—" I made a vow that I would never again look on a white man but to kill him!" He strode rapidly up and down before the council, his rifle on his arm. "Now I look about me in the camp and see white faces everywhere. They begin to get together in groups and talk and the next thing we know one of them will get away and bring trouble on us all. The blood in me boils when I remember that I have not kept that vow!"

He beat with his hand upon his chest.

"It's not the half-breeds I mean. They're our friends, our relations." He stopped, bent over and swept his arm in the faces of our little group. "*It's these white people I'm talking about!*"

I

The half-breeds seated among us edged quietly away ; soon not one remained within six feet of us. A look that aroused in me a sense of grave peril came into the eyes of the young men banded at the head of the circle as the war chief spoke. Some who had left their guns disappeared and returned with them. Tall Pine, one of Big Bear's band whom I had befriended frequently during the winter, came round, stretched himself on the grass behind me, seized my hand and pressed it.

" *N'Chawamis !* (My brother !)" he murmured in Cree.

I was touched. It meant that I had at least one friend among this cut-throat band, one champion who would defend me while breath lingered in his worn old body.

Wandering Spirit went on : " There's the Company's chief ! " He pointed at McLean. " When we wanted to get him out of the fort, him and his family, to save their lives, he was not willing to come. But when we offered to let the police, our enemies, off, he was not long in getting them out of the way. And they say he has heaps of ammunition hidden, too, and he won't give it to us ! "

Wandering Spirit when he said this knew that he lied, but he was trying to rouse the savage instincts of his followers to commit a second butchery. Those were moments, indeed, when, in the language of the Indians, " our hearts were on the ground."

But when the war chief finished and sat down, Big Bear rose and stretched out his hands over our heads.

"I pity every white man we have saved!" he cried, his voice tremulous with emotion. "Instead of speaking bad about them, give back to them some of the things you have taken. See; they are poor! Naked! And they are not, like us, often hungry; they do not know how the teeth of the cold bites! They have always worn warm clothes. Have pity!"

Little Poplar followed the chief. With his arms folded and his head bent over them in a posture of endearment, he said, smiling, in his high-pitched voice: "I look upon the children of the Company's chief as my own. Do them no harm!"

To our intense relief, the council in another few minutes dissolved and we returned in safety to our tents. But had Wandering Spirit found one or two to support him in fanning the incendiary spark, we should never have quitted our seats alive.

CHAPTER XVI

DAYS IN CAMP

THE heavy snow that came on the night that Fort
Pitt fell soon melted and the glory of the North-
west spring covered the land. How we joyed in
those bright warm days, so full of light and promise
if only this dreadful time should pass ! The yellow
grass of the old year, turning so quickly that one
could almost see the change to brilliant green; the
murmur of the creeks; the boom of rending ice;
the straining of the buds in their sheaths ; the twitter
of the birds; the hum of insect life—all helped us
to shake off the depression that had well-nigh over-
whelmed us and to take a fresh interest in existence.
Our captors, too, began to look with more friendly
eyes upon us and our danger seemed to grow less.
We obtained more freedom and wandered farther
from the lodges. Came a day when guns were even
loaned to Stanley Simpson and myself and we made
occasional short hunting excursions in the after-
noons with some of the Indians.

Shortly after the Indians returned from Pitt,
camp was moved two miles to a position commanding from flanking hills a view of the surrounding country, the camp itself being hidden by belts
of spruce.

An ambitious youth named The Wolf had con-
trived a buckboard out of two pairs of horse-rake
wheels, the property of the Indian department,
connected by a platform of boards nailed securely

to the front and rear axles, on which he had mounted a soap-box seat. The maiden cruise of this ship of the wilderness for ever blasted the aspirations of the designer to the rôle of a master of the carriage-builder's craft. Such a thing as a straight trail was unknown in the Frog Lake region, and with its rigid axles his carriage would move in only two directions—straight ahead or straight back. The Wolf's first attempt to follow the trail furnished his friends much hilarity. His buckboard persisted in laying out a trail of its own, and when he swung his pony to the right the vehicle turned over on his head. The pony bolted. Later The Wolf recovered the pony and the shafts. He had spent a whole week making his buckboard and got just five minutes' utility out of it.

Our new camp was near Frog Lake. Huge blocks of crumbling ice from the lake were running in its channel and the Indians told us the stream was full of pike. Stanley Simpson and I got permission to go fishing. We drove down with Louis Patenaude to the ruins of the settlement.

It was a month after the massacre and I had not visited the spot since that terrible day in the beginning of April. And what a change presented itself to me ! Where was all the quiet, home-like charm of that beautiful landscape ? There were the charred ruins of the buildings. Before what had been Delaney's house lay the head of poor Tom Quinn's little brown-and-white cocker, the dog he had been at such pains to train and whose clever tricks were his pride and delight. Death and desolation now. That was all.

Among the ashes of the stables we found the iron

parts of some pitchforks and turned back to camp. Patenaude followed the trail down which Dill, my former partner, and Gilchrist had been chased and overhauled by the Indians on that fatal day, and in a slight hollow rimmed by wooded hills, lying in the middle of the trail, where he had been shot down beside his master, we came across Gilchrist's black-and-white dog. Off to the right in the grass beside the trees lay the bodies of the two men, left unburied by command of the Indians. Louis had pulled up close to them. It was a horrible sight. I held my breath. " For heaven's sake, Louis, drive on ! " I muttered.

At the camp Simpson and I fixed poles in the pitchfork irons and went to the creek to spear fish. Discarding our shoes, trousers rolled above our knees, we tramped up and down in the icy water. The shallows swarmed pike. We drove them into corners, caught them on the forks and tossed them on the bank. Within an hour we had forty and returned to camp. Supper that night was a feast. While the pike is supposed to be somewhat flavourless, the change from a steady diet of beef was most agreeable. Louis had secured tea, sugar, rice and flour at Pitt and his wife made excellent bread.

Let me attempt the difficult task of describing the Cree Grass or War Dance as I saw it day after day in Big Bear's camp:

On a fine afternoon, Kahneepotaytayo, the head dancer or whipper-in, made the round of the lodges to summon the warriors to the dancing or soldiers' lodge, erected in each camp of three or four ordinary ones commandeered from their owners. The families so signalized for attention were presumed to regard the deprivation as an honour and sought shelter under their carts or in some adjacent bluff of poplar.

Kahneepotaytayo is decked in all his finery. His limbs are bare but for the bands of fur about knees and elbows and streaked with white mud. Broad bracelets of shining brass encircle his wrists. A crossbelt of bells hangs upon one shoulder and across his chest and smaller strings about his ankles jingle melodiously as he walks. He wears beaded moccasins and about his hips and the upper parts of his muscular thighs is fixed his fancy breechcloth. The royal skin of a silver fox trails down his back. His eyes form the centre of stars from which radiate shafts of black and yellow paint. Sable bars alternate with the vermilion on his bronze cheeks, while from his mouth to his throat is perfect blackness. A bunch of jet-tipped eagle plumes bristles from behind his blue-black plaited hair. His hand grasps a staff, to one end of which is bound with beaded red cloth a sword and to the other more feathers. So much of the blade is covered that only a foot of it is visible.

The drum begins its swelling beat and the dancers assemble. They seat themselves in a circle inside the great dancing lodge, one end of which is open. The drum looks like a large wooden grain-measure, the ends covered with parchment painted half black, half red. Around it sit the six drummers, beating a steady even beat and chanting the war song. Their faces wear a look of expectancy—the ceremony of Spearing the White Dog's Head is about to begin.

Kahneepotaytayo and his understudy are seated

a little apart. As the chant commences he rises and walks toward the centre of the circle. The women appear carrying the huge copper pot in which the dog strangled for the occasion is still simmering. They set it down beside the centre-pole and retire, for none but warriors may dance in the Grass Dance.

Kahneepotaytayo kneels before the kettle, his understudy beside him. The chant is a weird and slow one. The palms of the chief actors are outspread on the hard smooth earth, their bodies thrown forward on them, their staffs planted in front. The chant rises, and to the rhythmic beat of the drum falls gradually until the lowest strain, a deep bass, is reached and dwelt upon. Thence it jumps abruptly to the shrill beginning, and again it falls, gradually, to the bass. Again it jumps to the treble, to sink once more—and again.

See the painted and befeathered Kahneepotaytayo ! His lithe figure begins to sway, back and forth from side to side in time with the chant and his palms to rub lightly the damp bare soil. He raises and brushes them softly together, muttering some incantation—for it is a religious ceremony—then drops and moves them over the earth again. The chant grows faster, changing to the Horse Song; he springs suddenly to his feet and begins to dance. His eyes flash. The thews and sinews of his limbs and chest stand out like ropes or roll and ripple beneath the smooth coppery skin like the coils of a moving snake.

He circles about the White Dog's Head as though it were an enemy ready to strike should he approach too near—darts away with a shrill war-cry, crouching along the ground, all the while keeping step to the measured *pom ! pom ! pom ! pom !* of the big drum and the wild plaintive voices of the drummers. His body leans and sways, pitches and glides, as he draws nearer to the kettle, with all the grace and agility of a panther stealing upon its prey. His companion is close behind, his shadow in the flesh, doubling his every motion. Sweat pours from their dark satin skins and glistens on their naked painted limbs and chests and faces. The eagle plumes on Kahneepotaytayo's head toss with the twistings of his body. His eyes glow fiercely in the warm light. His face is set and drawn.

He creeps nearer the kettle. He lifts his spear, and with a swift bound launches it at the head of the White Dog. The drum stops. He draws himself up, places his fingers over his lips and a long piercing staccato yell echoes through the camp. It is the *coup*—the death. He raises the kettle and carries it three times round in a circle. A roar of applause comes from the seated warriors and a volley rolls from the big drum. Then he walks over, takes Wandering Spirit by the wrist and conducts him to a seat upon a blanket set apart for the councillors and goes back for Four-Sky Thunder, Little Poplar and Nopahchass. These are first served from the kettle ; afterward it is passed to the other dancers and all give their attention to the feast—the food of warriors.

The feasting over, dancing, in which all now join, is resumed. The drummers again start the Horse Song, echoing the steps of a horse at a smart trot. Kahneepotaytayo springs to his feet; he dances round the circle before the other dancers, spurring them with guttural cries of " *Hy-aw-aw !* " afoot, holding the whip he has exchanged for his sword threateningly over their heads. They rise as he passes and soon all are moving in a bewildering maze, shuffling along the ground bent double, turning suddenly as though attacked from behind, shouting shrill war-cries and otherwise imitating their old habits and practices in time of war. Abruptly the drum stops and they walk back to their places to rest. When held at night the weird effect of the dance was heightened.

Wandering Spirit was always conspicuous in the Grass Dance. Between the intervals of dancing it is customary for the distinguished warriors to " count their *coups* "—to tell off the scalps they have taken and the horses they have stolen from the enemy.

One fine afternoon shortly after Fort Pitt, I listened to the war chief count his *coups*. It was in one of the intervals of rest. With a motion of his hand, he started the drummers. Leaping to his feet, he danced toward the drum, rifle in hand, crouching and wheeling, much as Kahneepotaytayo had done in spearing the Dog's Head. Brilliant paints covered his face and the plaits of his curling black hair were bound with strips of otter fur. He looked ferocious as he danced stealthily toward the booming drum, swinging his rifle now here, now there, retreating and advancing again.

A small willow stick lay beside the drum. Presently he picked this up, crouched nearer and nearer and at length tossed it with a war whoop among the sticks of the drummers. The drumming ceased and the war chief drew himself up and began

to speak. He numbered off the Blackfoot—eleven,
I think—he had slain, pointing with his rifle in the
direction of each successive exploit.

" And then," he concluded, " there were another
and another." (No names were mentioned, but
he referred I knew to Indian Agent Quinn and
Father Fafard.) " *How! Aywaik! Ahnis, N'kee-
saynewin!* (So ! That's something ! I'm getting
old, you see !)" he added with a laugh.

The dancing lodge is also the soldiers' lodge.
The war chief was head soldier, or commander,
and his followers the soldiers. Such laws as were
ordained for the regulation of the camp were en-
forced by the soldiers' lodge. Occasionally it
became necessary to discipline refractory members
of the band.

One afternoon I was standing near the soldiers'
lodge, watching the dance, when Oskatask, a Big
Bear Indian, came down the trail close by. At a
word from the war chief, Kahneepotaytayo and his
assistant, knives in their hands, jumped to their
feet, ran out, caught Oskatask by either arm and
marched him into the dancing lodge. He was
much older, bigger and more powerful than either
of the young bucks, but beyond a sullen protest
he made no show of insubordination. He stood
expostulating before the war chief, but his harangue
had no effect upon Wandering Spirit. He sat with
the face of a sphinx and heard him to the end,
while the young men stood with a hand on either
shoulder of the speaker, their long naked blades
in their other hands. Then Wandering Spirit
gestured, and they turned and with the knives
sliced the blanket coat of the prisoner to ribbons.

Oskatask stood as if carved in stone. Had he
stirred his flesh also would have been in ribbons.
They released him then and he stalked away, his
face black with smothered fury.

He had killed cattle belonging to another Indian.
This was his punishment.

On another afternoon some time later the soldiers
gave the camp a general shaking-up.

Some of the warriors, apparently tired of the
endless dancing, had disregarded the formal sum-
mons to the dancing lodge. I was standing before
Patenaude's tent. I heard a chorus of yells and
looking up saw the soldiers coming on the run
around the wide circle enclosed by the camp. They
carried knives and axes. They stopped before a
lodge, and in a moment slashed it to shreds, while
the inmates sat cowed and in no little danger as
their habitation fell about their ears. Then the
soldiers snatched furs and blankets from about their
trembling owners and cut or tore them to bits in
their teeth as they ran on to the next lodge singled
out for discipline. In this way they destroyed in a
few minutes no less than ten lodges, but the attend-
ance at the dances was for some time materially
improved. The soldiers stayed in the dancing lodge
all night and took turns in acting as guards to the
camp, to prevent the escape of white prisoners and
anticipate surprise by troops.

When word was given to strike camp and march,
a fair interval was allowed for compliance with
the order. Then, Wandering Spirit leading, the
soldiers marched around the camp and assisted the
tardy ones to take down their lodges. This they
did by lifting the lodge bodily from over the heads

of its inmates and laying it flat on the ground some distance away.

At length the carts are packed and the caravan moves. One by one the carts fall into line, sending up a creaking chorus from the wooden axles audible miles away on the prairie, until all have left camp. Up and down the long train ride the chiefs and headmen, waking the laggards and preserving order. Here rides Wandering Spirit on a tall gaunt grey mare taken from the Indian department at Onion Lake, her flanks plentifully striped with white mud and her foretop and tail ornamented with tufts of feathers. The war chief wears his lynx-skin cap, a whole skin, head fixed to tail, open at the top, making a huge double loop of long grey fur. The five eagle plumes, for each of which he boasts he means to have a white man's scalp, float above the cap. Thrown loosely about his shoulders is his long blue-and-white blanket coat. Green cloth leggings cover his legs and beaded moccasins his feet. His sheath knife shows in his belt of yellow cartridges. His right hand holds lightly the slack bridle-rein and in the crook of his left arm rests his Winchester—the rifle commandeered from Henry Quinn at Pitt.

Young bucks, two on a pony, dash in and out through the line, followed by the imprecations of old wrinkled women, toiling painfully along with bent shoulders, dragging by cords dejected-looking curs which are also beasts of burden and pull travoys. Some are hunting ducks and rabbits among the numerous bluffs and lakes along the route. Seated in the carts on rolls of bedding, tepees, lodge poles, boxes and provisions are the squaws, and papooses embracing the inevitable family puppies.

Here goes another old woman, leading a pony with a travoy—a contrivance formed of two poles lashed together near their tops, the angle thus engineered resting across the pony's back, the butts dragging on the ground in the rear. Behind the horse and a couple of feet from the earth the load is fixed—blackened kettles and pans, with perhaps an infant in a mossbag filling the biggest of the kettles. Here a young and pretty squaw perches above the travoy, astride the pony's back. Or perhaps her feet are crossed on the ample seat like a Turk's. The half-naked boys are scattered along the train, yelling and shooting arrows to keep the loose animals up and the caravan in motion.

Now a cart collapses and the line comes together like an accordion. An old woman ties her dog by the leading cord to the wheel of the cart in front and shambles off to a seat under a bluff to rest and smoke. Presently the line starts again. The ancient crone tumbles forward shrilling " *Tesqua!—tesqua!* " at the top of her cracked old voice. Her dog is being hanged on his leading line by the great revolving wooden wheel. But suddenly the rotten cord breaks and he comes down with a clatter among his load of kettles and pans and howling terrified infant. The long train stretches out once more like an uncoiling snake. Everywhere there is a glint of gun barrels, a reckless galloping to and fro, a lowing of cattle, a waving of blankets, shouts, dust and confusion.

A halt is made at noon, the kettle is boiled for tea and the animals are loosed to feed on the rich

grass. Then the march is resumed and goes on
till evening. The lodges are pitched in a great
circle, each with its camp fire, and the dancing lodge
near the centre. Night and darkness fall, but not
silence. The drum booms from the red walls of the
dancing lodge, the sneaking dogs snarl and scuffle
over the scraps tossed from the tents, perhaps a
shot goes off by accident sending a hard chilling
note through the camp's drowsing voices. Four-Sky
Thunder, painkiller drugged, trolls tipsily in a
near-by lodge. From another the sound of a gambling
song rises. The half-Blackfoot chief stalks through
the camp, crying his dolorous wailing chant because
there is bad blood between the bands. He is trying
to exorcise the devils that have caused it.

Wearied, I at length drop into a troubled sleep.
But suddenly I find myself bolt upright on my
blanket. My heart is beating not at all. But
presently it starts again, very slowly, the halted
blood resumes its flow and I fall back and close my
eyes once more. A horse has stumbled against the
taut guy-ropes of the lodge, that is all, and they
snap like whips in my startled ear. But it might
have been a painted man, entering stealthily with
a knife in his teeth and murder in his heart.

CHAPTER XVII

AN INDIAN CANNIBAL

LONE MAN was always my friend and one bright afternoon in early May I walked to his tent to smoke and chat with the son-in-law of Big Bear. The usual dance was on, but Lone Man seldom attended. The Indians still had the Hudson's Bay Company's flag—the Union Jack with the old corporation's crest in the corner—and I noted with satisfaction that the ensign flew at half-mast and upside down above the dancing lodge. I fancied it might be an omen of impending woe for the soldiers.

Lone Man invited me to a seat on the floor of his lodge. He asked me, according to his custom, endless questions concerning the number and ways of the white men, in which he displayed the keenest interest. Little Poplar and his son-in-law, a Crow from Montana, came in and the host set before us bowls of dripping and sheaves of dried meat, which we ate. It tasted very good.

I noticed Big Bear's men unusually in evidence, carrying their guns and wearing grave faces. An ominous quiet reigned. When his tribal friends were gone, I asked Lone Man to enlighten me.

" Well," said he, " you have heard of the old woman in camp who wants to eat human flesh. She says if she isn't dead before the sun goes out to-night she cannot be killed and will then begin to eat the children. They are afraid. She has but half a smoke to live. Come, we will go and see her."

At the farther end of the camp we came to a lodge around which were grouped many of Big Bear's warriors. Wandering Spirit in full war dress was there with his Winchester. His look was inexorable, relentless. Four-Sky Thunder stood near him. The doomed woman, the *weetigo*, crouched on the floor of the lodge groaning and mumbling to herself, a poor demented creature, a helpless, aged and ailing imbecile. We had tried to persuade the Indians that nothing serious was wrong, that she could do them no harm—we saw, now, unavailingly. We suggested that they give her laudanum, as an easier way to the Sand Hills. Unfortunately, no one had any of the drug.

As Lone Man and I stood with the crowd looking in at her, Henry Quinn and Malcolm Macdonald approached under an escort of Indians. The crowd made way for them. Quinn knelt beside the old woman and bound her wrists and ankles. Then she was placed on a tanned beef-hide, Quinn took a corner, Macdonald another, Indians the remaining two and the wretched invalid was borne to the place of death, an open space a few hundred yards from the lodge. They set her down on the skin, blind-folded her and an old half-breed named Charlebois, the lower half of his face painted black, leaped toward her brandishing a heavy club.

" You have asked everybody to kill her and all were afraid. Don't laugh at me for striking a woman, and don't say I did it ! " he cried.

He swung the club and struck her a frightful blow on the temple. She fell forward, blood gushing from her mouth. A boy named Bright Eyes stepped out and shot the senseless skull. Afterward it was

K

severed from the trunk. The body was flung into a well and the battered head burned on a pile of brush. The superstitious savages were determined there should be no possibility of the resurrection of the *weetigo.*

I should say for myself that I was not a witness of this diabolical proceeding. I heard the shooting and saw the smoke of the fire, but learned these particulars later. As to the part played by Quinn, it was forced upon him by the Big Bear miscreants.

Insanity in Indians, oddly enough, often takes this form of would-be cannibalism.

CHAPTER XVIII

THE North American Indian is an incorrigible gamester. The passion for play seems to be born with him. Since the advent of the white man he has learned to gamble with cards, but long before he ever saw the paleface he had his own rude games of chance. In Big Bear's camp one might see gathered on any bright day in the shade of a cart an excited circle—a group of gamblers surrounded by their partisans. Let us take a look at them:

Two men are seated opposite each other on the ground with blankets over their knees. Each has beside him an assistant or partner, and a pile of articles of more or less value which he is prepared from time to time to offer as stakes. Two bits of wood an inch and a half long are the gambler's cards.

The player of the side having the sticks at the time takes them in his hands, his partner picks up a small drum the size and shape of a milk pan, holding it by parchment strings stretched across its open back and begins to sing, accompanying himself on the drum. The feet of the gambler are doubled up beneath him. He puts his hands beneath the blanket across his knees, brings them out, closed, and in time with the song jolts in his seat like a man in the saddle, bends his head, throws it back, uttering a continual sharp " *Chug-chug! chug-chug!* " somewhat like the steam exhaust of a tugboat. Sometimes he opens a hand, displaying one of the sticks or else showing that it is empty. Again the hand dives beneath the blanket and comes out, perhaps with the stick, perhaps not. He folds his arms on his chest; he flings them out, flashing the hands open and shut. All the while the steady chugging comes from between his teeth and the body jolts up and down. If he is expert the sticks may be passed or shot openly between the hands so dexterously that the opposing players may not see them, though they are generally exchanged under the blanket.

Meanwhile his opponent sits smoking and watching him intently. All the contortions of his *vis-à-vis* are intended to mislead him. His purpose is to divine correctly where the two sticks are at any given time—whenever he may choose to hazard a guess. If the guess is correct the sticks pass to the other side and a marker is stuck in the sod to represent points added to the number needed to win the stakes then being played for. If he misses the same side retains the sticks and adds a marker to its row, the stakes being put up at so many sticks or markers. The sticks may be both beneath the blanket, both in one hand, or one in either hand. Again, one may be under the blanket and the other in either hand. It is a hard matter for the guesser to recover the sticks once they have passed to a clever opponent. The hands of the juggler are always opened and the sticks shown when a guess is hazarded, to prove it either right or wrong. If right, the sticks are at once tossed over.

Occasionally the guesser receives advice and

suggestions from his assistant and guesses accordingly. Or he may be staked, as a white man stakes a novice to play for him at faro or roulette. Signs are the language of the Indian gamester. He claps the back of one hand in the palm of the other, holding up one or two fingers according to his guess. It depends on which hand he thinks holds the sticks which fingers he holds up, those of the left or right hand. If he thinks both sticks are beneath the blanket, he makes a different sign with both fingers down.

Anything he owns may be hazarded—bedding, rifle, knife, moccasins, pipe, tobacco, saddle, horse. He may lose all—may even rise at the last, pull off his shirt and stake it—but he never murmurs. He is hardly a philosopher; he is merely improvident, reckless, a natural gambler. He laughs when he has nothing more to lose and goes away singing, with a jest over his shoulder. The excitement pleases him and satisfies his passion for play. He likes to bewilder his opponent, to show his dexterity in juggling the sticks and little he cares whether he wins or loses. He will not starve, nor will he lack a smoke while there is tobacco or food in the camp. He will simply drop into the lodge nearest his.

Indians in time of war have various methods of signalling. The two in most common use were fire and mirrors. The smoke of the signal fire, built on a commanding height, might be seen for many miles in the clear atmosphere of the prairie. At night the glow itself or its reflection in the sky was equally serviceable. By this method intelligence was carried unbelievable distances in a short time.

There is little doubt that Big Bear's band was apprised through signal fires of the Duck Lake fight and the half-breed outbreak, two hundred miles away, within twenty-four hours of the engagement, while we the whites at Frog Lake did not hear of it for some days. Of course the fires must have relation to some event anticipated.

Mirrors are available only in bright weather and for comparatively short distances, though even flashes from a small mirror may be seen in favourable country for many miles. A given number of flashes conveys definite information of some kind. I have seen Big Bear's band thrown into a state of feverish excitement, men rushing for their guns, women talking and gesticulating, by a series of flashes telegraphed from a distance of at least five miles.

A word here about the sign language in use among all the Plains Indians. It is a mistake to suppose that there is any similarity between the languages of the various stocks. The Blackfeet, Bloods and Peigans are of the same parent stock and their speech is therefore practically one. The same is true of the Crees, Chippewas and Salteaux; of the Sioux, Cheyennes and the Dakotahs, Stonies or Assiniboines; and of the Chippewyans, Sarcees and Apaches. But a Blackfoot, generally, speaking his own language to a Cree, Sioux, Apache or Crow would have as much chance of being understood as if he were addressing a Hairy Ainu in English. For example, take the simple little English word "No." In Blackfoot it is *sa*, in Cree *namoya*, in Chippewyan *eeli* and in Assiniboine *wanitch*.

The Blackfoot gets round the difficulty by "speaking signs." The fingers of both hands intertwined represent a lodge (crossed poles at top) or a house (log). Sleep is symbolized by placing the head sidewise on the palm of the hand. Numbers are recorded by holding up fingers; opening and shutting the hands once means ten—ten times, one hundred. Closing the hand and opening it suddenly with the fingers extended signifies shooting —the flying shot pellets. Rubbing the palm of one hand on the palm of the other means to " wipe out " (annihilation). The index finger of each hand crooked on either side of the head in the shape of horns suggests the buffalo or cattle.

An Indian comes into a trading post and asks for evaporated apples by touching his ear—it resembles a ring of the packed fruit. Or a front tooth—beans. Each tribe has a sign. The Sioux is the cut-throat—a finger drawn under the chin. The Cree sign is two tongues; two fingers pushed straight out from the mouth—liar. The Peigan publishes his nationality in an alien camp by rubbing his cheek with his fist—he is a painted face. The Crow moves his hands like the wings of a bird. The sign for the Snake Indian is readily suggested by a motion of the hand. The tribal sign for the Apache is not printable.

And so on. There are signs for riding, smoking, baking, boiling, hearing, fighting, running, seeing, eating, drinking; for anger, drunkenness, sorrow, hunger, thirst, weariness, insanity; for the sun, moon, stars, day, night, rain, wind, heat, cold; for birth, life, death—in fact a good sign-talker can speak far more fluently with his hands than many an educated white man can with his tongue. I have seen a Saskatchewan Cree and a Nez Perce from the Columbia seated side by side on the ground, converse for an hour, telling stories of the chase, of love and of war, without speaking a word. It was one of the most graceful, impressive and interesting conversations I ever listened to. Also the quietest.

The paints in use by the Indians also have their significance. The bright vermilion is a holiday paint and denotes cheerfulness in the wearer. The blue is used mainly by way of contrast, in forming stars and emblems upon the features. The yellow is the real war paint. A few moments before the massacre at Frog Lake, Wandering Spirit appeared with his eyelids and lips thickly coated with yellow ochre. It gave him a look of unspeakable hideousness, and was without doubt the signal for the commencement of the tragedy.

Black is the death colour, and in the evening after the massacre the lower parts of the faces of all who took part in it were painted this sombre hue.

CHAPTER XIX

MORE DAYS IN CAMP

SPRING came on apace; the days grew warm. About the camp raced the boys, the younger nude, shooting with bow and arrows at gophers and marks or rolling in the dust with wolfish puppies. Here gambols a youngster with bare legs, about whose brown little body is wrapped a mounted policeman's brass-buttoned scarlet tunic, secured at Pitt. Outside this, hanging about his hips, is hooked a pair of ladies' corsets, got by his father at the same place and time. He is a quaint picture as he frisks about with a ready bow, the envy of his playmates.

An ancient redskin passes near them. He wears a very dark, ragged and dirty blanket folded about his stooped shoulders, and on his head a nice clean freshly-pipe-clayed military helmet. He feels that he is elegantly attired and as is befitting his gait is stately and solemn. He and the youngsters are on the same intellectual plane.

As time passed and we grew perhaps in the general esteem of the Indians, they were ready to provide both Stanley Simpson and myself with wives. Lone Man, with whom Simpson lived, was particularly anxious that he should marry his young daughter. Simpson got round the difficulty I believe by telling him he already had a wife and being a white man, his principles would not allow him to take another. My defence was poverty— one of the most dependable, year-round, hard-working defences of which I have any knowledge.

153

When a dog-feast was held and there was a likelihood of the prisoners being invited to partake, I tried to keep out of sight. It is a grave affront to refuse to eat when an Indian places food of whatever kind before one. After Big Bear had spoken, urging that some of our clothing be returned to us, the camp one day gave a dog-feast and asked the prisoners to attend. The Indians' commendable purpose was to give them bedding and clothing. I saw Kahneepotaytayo coming to ask the whites, but I had rather get along with the rags I wore and the one cowskin I slept on than receive all the blankets and wearing apparel in the world at the price of eating stewed dog. It is probably delicious, but I imagine one has to cultivate a taste for it. Nursing this idea, I kept carefully out of the way of the head dancer, slipping from lodge to lodge and finally doubling back and eluding him altogether. However, the Indians were good enough to set apart a blanket for me, notwithstanding my studied avoidance of their intended hospitality. It came useful a little later when I had to guard Louis Patenaude's horses at night.

A few weeks after coming into camp Stanley Simpson had an attack of quinsy. His throat was so swollen and inflamed that he could eat no solid food and for several days had almost starved. Then Lone Man's wife came to him one evening with a bowl of broth. Simpson was ravenous; intense yearning filled his eyes as he sniffed at it. The aroma was most intriguing. Still, he hesitated. He wished most ardently to drink it, yet he feared to ask questions and he did not dare touch it without. And he might not care for it when he got an answer.

"What's it made of?" he said at length desperately.

"Meat," said Mrs. Lone Man, non-committally.

"That must mean beef," Simpson observed thoughtfully.

"Smells nice—looks all right," I remarked encouragingly. I was glad to see one of the dearest friends I ever had want to take something, no matter what. And he drank—drank it with relish. A moment later Mrs. Lone Man said with a grin:

"I suppose you don't know what it was?"

Simpson looked up in alarm. He shook his head.

"Well," said the warm-hearted lady; "dog soup."

And Simpson went out with a rush and parted with his broth in much mental and physical anguish.

We were moving camp. Stanley Simpson and I had been walking near the tail of the procession and arriving at the new camp-ground we found some lodges already pitched. Occasionally an Indian lacking transportation left his lodge poles at one camp and cut others when he reached the next.

We crossed a poplar bluff near the new camp. Some of the Indians were cutting poles and Catfish, a Chippewyan, made a feint of slashing at my legs as we passed him. The axe swung uncomfortably near. The move was quite unexpected and naturally I jumped. This amused Catfish—and pleased him also; I was easily scared, he said. It was a great thing to scare a white man. I said nothing, but I made a mental note of the incident. Some day I hoped to repay Catfish in a way he mightn't like. The chance came sooner than I had looked for. Catfish was a tireless braggart, so I knew him to be a coward. However, policy still demanded that we treat such pleasantries on the part of our captors as jokes. Later, the demands of policy were less exacting. We began to know our men.

We were camped on the bank of the Pipestone. A group of Indians one morning were amusing themselves " pulling sticks." I was resting on my back in the grass near them with my knees drawn up. Other prisoners lounged about.

The game is a simple one. Two men sit on the ground, facing, their knees bent and the soles of their feet opposed. Their arms rest on their knees and their hands grasp a round stick two feet long, held fairly between them above their feet. At a signal both pull, until one is lifted or hauled over by the other. It is a simple test of strength though there is a knack to it.

Catfish came over, leaned across my legs and pushing me with the stick, invited me to try my back against his. I did not care for the game and told him so. He persisted. I jolted him slightly with a foot. He flared up and grabbed me round the knees. Then I, too, became earnest. I drew my feet back suddenly and planted them in the Chippewyan's chest. I happened to be wearing boots that morning. Catfish described a complete parabola off the back of his neck, and I rose and looked at him smilingly as he got up, sputtering and coughing, some distance away.

Halpin expostulated in an undertone. He said I was indiscreet and I expect he was right; anyway, I told him some things I might better have left unsaid. Catfish looked displeased. He mumbled several uncomplimentary epithets and concluded by remarking that he might very likely kill me. I told him to come and I would save him the trouble by reversing the programme. He did not come, and I reminded him that he had once told me I was easily scared. The Wood Crees laughed— humiliation of humiliations ! And the prestige and pride of Catfish, chief brave of the Chippewyans, were irretrievably damaged.

Later, I took occasion to impress upon General Strange and a board of inquiry what a good Indian Catfish was. I do not think Catfish appreciated my interest.

I was standing one day outside Patenaude's lodge when an Indian came up and taking my arm, led me to an open space between the lodges. He pointed to some animals grazing a short way off.

" You see that white horse ? " he asked. I nodded. " That's the one I was riding when I told you to go on, I didn't want to hurt you."

" I'm not likely to forget him," I replied.

He was the Indian I had seen chasing the half-breed Goulet with a gun during the massacre; Goulet had given him the horse to spare his life. Later, in dread of what seemed imminent death at his hands, I had come face to face with this Indian riding the horse, and for some reason which I am unable even to-day to guess at, he had permitted me to continue walking instead of stretching me lifeless at his feet. So I expressed my sense of deep gratitude for his unquestioned magnanimity.

As the days grew long, Stanley Simpson and myself obtained permission to leave camp and hunt in the woods and lakes abounding everywhere along the Saskatchewan. We borrowed guns from our keepers and were put on our parole not to attempt escape. For that matter, and for reasons already stated, we had no thought of making such an attempt. Many a long afternoon we tramped about together, as we had done often before in happier times, enjoying the glorious spring of the North-west and escaping for a few hours the unrelished society of our savage hosts. The ducks, prairie chickens, rabbits and occasional eggs we brought home gave us a welcome change from our usual bill of fare.

Simpson was the most enthusiastic sportsman I ever knew. He would wade into the cold water of a slough to his neck, holding his gun high, and stand like a post, only his head showing, for half an hour, on the chance of getting a shot at a duck that had had the perversity to keep beyond range of the shore. I had always considered my love of sport above the average, but it never carried me to such lengths as did that of that prince of good fellows, Stanley Simpson.

We had been out a mile or two from camp one afternoon and were strolling leisurely homeward. Nearing the lodges we met a number of Indians riding furiously toward the Saskatchewan River, the north bank of which lay not far distant. We saw at once that something unusual was in the wind. Could the troops we were expecting have been reported? At the camp a few minutes later we quickly learned the reason for the excitement. Henry Quinn and Pierre Blondin were missing—it was believed they were attempting to escape! The situation looked dark for them should they be caught. It also looked dark for us who remained, for the Indians had repeatedly declared that if one prisoner escaped they would kill all the others.

We spent a bad quarter of an hour; then the Indians returned with the fugitives. For they had been fugitives. They were taken into Pritchard's tent. Big Bear's soldiers gathered at the door outside, armed and in anything but a peaceful mood. It had grown dusk. I was standing near, awaiting developments, when Patenaude came up to me, his gun on his arm, and said roughly:

" Go to my tent and stay there ! "

Never before had he spoken to me in such a fashion and I obeyed immediately, for I knew he must have a reason. He came in an hour later and explained: Big Bear's band had been determined to kill the fugitives but the Wood Crees once more stepped in and saved them. Kahweechetwaymot entered Pritchard's tent, sat down before Quinn and began to polish his revolver with a silk handkerchief.

" Go outside to-night and I will shoot you ! " he told Quinn. A moment later, when things looked darkest, two Wood Crees of the Saddle Lake band came with their guns and announced that they intended to protect Quinn. " If you harm him it means war between the Wood and Plain Crees," was their ultimatum.

Big Bear's men, for all their swagger, were not willing to risk war. The Wood Indians stayed all night with Quinn. Louis explained to me that I had been in danger outside. In case of trouble he wanted me out of harm's way.

Our amusements in camp were not sufficiently numerous or distracting to keep us up late at night.

In some way I do not now remember I had managed to secure again the violin I had had at Frog Lake. It helped to pass the time. Then Simpson and I visited the McLeans often in their tents and passed many an hour pleasantly that would otherwise have crawled, chatting with Mr. and Mrs. McLean and their daughters. Having no books we could not read and so smoked the more. Four-Sky Thunder kept me in tobacco. Lone Man had a beautiful meerschaum pipe that had belonged to Father Marchand, the murdered priest, I owned a nice briar which Lone Man coveted and we exchanged. The meerschaum I gave later to Senator Girard, of Manitoba.

Lone Man was an unwavering friend of mine. He said that when the cruel war was over he would take me and go across country to the Missouri River, the land of the Kitchemokoman. I should take a position there with a trading company and he would camp close by. I could live with him and furnish the tea and provisions for the family. As Simpson had refused his daughter, I might have her. The picture was an alluring one and I did not think it necessary at the time to inform him that I was too modest to think I might be able to fill such a prominent place in it.

" *N'chawamis*," said Lone Man one day, " when the soldiers come I will give you a rifle and you will fight with us against them."

I said my aim was poor. There were Indians in camp without rifles who would be capable of much more effective work; he had better loan it to them. I had a violin and while the fighting was in progress I would furnish the music. Doubtless the troops

would have a band and it wouldn't do to show that
we were behind them in any way. I think Lone
Man accepted my views. At all events he did not
offer to supply me with a weapon when the troops
under General Strange arrived.

Mrs. Delaney and Mrs. Gowanlock rode with
Pritchard on his wagon when camp was moved.
The McLeans were allowed to borrow a team to
pull their belongings. Many of the children in
their big family were very young and it was not
always possible for everybody to ride. Patenaude
sometimes gave me a seat on his wagon which
I resigned to one of the McLeans. When it became
necessary to abandon the wagons after the Frenchman's Butte battle, the situation was made harder
for Mrs. McLean and the girls. They were obliged
to walk and not infrequently to carry the toddlers
of the family on their backs.

Little Poplar, early in our captivity, wished to
add the two eldest girls to his seraglio. He had only
six wives. It was amusing and somewhat alarming.
I do not know how the difficulty was got round
but he was in some manner induced to forgo his
polygamous inclinations in so far as white wives
were concerned.

Hodson, a stocky, pockmarked, cross-eyed little
Englishman who wore glasses and had been the
McLeans' cook at Pitt, was an object of special
and peculiar interest to the Indians. They appeared
to regard him as some new variety of grub, and
I know they would have liked to kill him out of
mere idle curiosity to see him squirm. I wonder
they did not do it, but he lived to hang some of
them later.

L

CHAPTER XX

For weeks Big Bear's men had tried to persuade the Wood Crees to move toward Battleford and join Poundmaker. James K. Simpson and I had secretly opposed this.

" They killed the white people," we told the Wood Crees, " not you. Let them go. You stop. When the soldiers come we will make peace for you. Big Bear's men say they will fight. Unless you separate, that will make it hard for us to help you."

There was no love lost between the factions, but our efforts were offset by some of the leaders, who stalked through the camp making night hideous with their dismal wailing, pleaded, tore their clothes, heaped dust on their heads, in their endeavour to hold the bands together. The Wood Crees would have been pleased enough to see the last of Big Bear and his men, but the others would not have it that way. Apparently the red-handed assassins got a sort of moral bracing from the association with their more respectable relatives that they were unwilling to be deprived of.

Blocked in one direction, we turned, aided by Fitzpatrick, in another. Our plan this time had in it the spice of danger, for it was nothing less than an attempt to incite the Wood Crees to make open war on Big Bear. How nearly we succeeded, what I am about to relate will show.

About the first of May the camp by short marches had begun to move toward Pitt. Big Bear's warriors continued to dance almost daily. Scouts had been sent to Poundmaker and returned with news of

the Cut Knife fight. I was sitting with Stanley
Simpson in Lone Man's lodge. The Indians, the
scouts said, after a long and hard battle had almost
been defeated, many of Poundmaker's men had
been killed and the band had moved away. They
added that a big body of soldiers from across the
Rockies was marching down the Saskatchewan to
attack Big Bear.

Lone Man flushed darkly as he listened to this.
He turned suddenly to me.

" *Kee topwaytin, chee ?* (You credit this, say ?)"
he asked. " It can't be true. The iron road (railway) across the mountains is not yet finished."

I replied evasively as usual, for I saw he wished
to disbelieve the news and I did not care to risk
offending him.

One afternoon a week later Big Bear's band
danced the war dance. The warriors marched in a
body round the inside of the great circle enclosed
by nearly two hundred lodges, squatting at intervals
before the lodges of the chiefs and headmen in a
little circle of their own. Simpson, Fitzpatrick and
I, with some Wood Crees, looked on.

" Why do you let Wandering Spirit and his men
kick you around as if you were dogs ? " we said to
them in whispers. " They are not more than
eighty armed; you number three times as many.
You don't want to go to Battleford, to join Riel,
to fight the soldiers, yet you let this handful of
murderers walk over you. Are you frightened ?
Look at them now—you could wipe them out in a
minute as they squat there, like they did the white
men at Frog Lake ! Why don't you do it ? They
are your enemies as well as ours. The government
would be glad. They would do more for you."

It was a perilous business for we might be betrayed and would pay with our lives. But life in the camp was becoming intolerably monotonous. We thought, too, that we knew our men, nor were we deceived. Our words took root. The idea budded and expanded into a conspiracy—of which more later.

Wandering Spirit rose and made a speech.

" Fourteen years ago when we fought the Blackfeet, the River-Men (Plain Crees) were afraid of nothing. When we heard the enemy was near we rushed to meet him, and you all know Kahpaypamahchakwayo. He was never behind. I look around me to-day and what do I see ? None of the faces I saw about me then—instead, the faces of young men. How will it be now ? It is because you asked me, you young fellows, that ashes is all that is left of Frog Lake—that I did what I did. I hope we see the Queen's soldiers soon. When they come you will hear me, Kahpaypamahchakwayo, calling, young fellows—you will hear me shout the war cry of the River-Men—and if any does not follow me, he shall die as the white men died at Frog Lake ! "

He struck the stock of his rifle with his hand and sat down.

We moved on down the trail and about May 15th reached the Saskatchewan near Pipestone Creek, two miles east of Pitt. The weather was beautiful, the days long and warm, the sun bright, the grass riotously luxuriant, the delicate foliage appearing on poplar and willow. All nature wore a livery of brilliant green.

Big Bear's band was still determined on joining Poundmaker; they had endeavoured to coerce the Wood Crees by firing Fort Pitt, destroying most of the provisions. But some buildings and the flour and bacon in them were saved, and their action served only to further provoke the Wood Crees. These desired to lay in a stock of food and one morning sent carts to the fort for loads.

James K. Simpson and I had kept alive the spark of resentment kindled in the breast of Cut Arm, one of the most discontented of the Wood Cree chiefs. He decidedly favoured ridding himself of his compromising associates.

"You speak good words," he said to us. "We did not wish to raise a gun against the white man. Our young men were forced into it by these dogs, and see how they treat us now ! They have taken our horses as they took yours, and with threats they rule the camp. They kill our cattle—the cattle we raised. They are not as brave as our own young men, but they have held them down with words. But wait a little. You will see ! "

We waited a good deal but without seeing much out of the usual. Nothing occurred. The Wood Crees had not been brought to the point of open defiance. Then came this day on which they went to Fort Pitt for provisions.

Oskatask was a Big Bear Indian. Gladieu, my Wood Cree friend, sat this morning on the grass before his lodge holding by a line his roan mare. She was a good mare. Oskatask came up.

"I'm going to the fort," he said. "Lend me your mare."

Gladieu knew some Plain Cree would want to borrow his mare and that if he lent her he would be just one good mare out. That was why he was holding her this fine May morning. He shook his head.

"I'm going to use her myself," he said.

Oskatask lowered his rifle and jabbed the muzzle in the Wood Cree's eye.

" *Muchastim !* " he muttered, and snatching the line out of Gladieu's hand he jumped on the horse and rode off.

Wandering Spirit witnessed this.   He had for some time divined that a rupture was imminent between the two factions and was doing all he could to prevent it.   In his new rôle of peacemaker, he went after his unruly follower, calling on him to stop.   Oskatask faced about and the two Indians —the one sullen, defiant; the other wrathful, threatening—with fingers on the locks of their guns—lowered for a moment on one another from beneath their war bonnets.

" Give up the mare, fool ! " said the war chief presently in a low voice.   " Do you want to bring war between us and these Wood Cree people ? We are not strong enough to beat them if they once will fight."

Oskatask held his ground stubbornly.   " I am riding to the fort.   I will return her after," he retorted.

Wandering Spirit raised his rifle.   " Give her back, dog ! " he said menacingly, advancing a step.

To temporize over compliance with the head soldier's order was to court instant death as Oskatask knew, but he took the chance.

" I said I would, didn't I ? " he returned belligerently.   " But when I'm ready—after a little."

He wheeled suddenly and with an eye over his shoulder, jammed his heels in the mare's ribs and clattered away toward Pitt.   Doubtless Oskatask recalled the day his coat had been slashed off his back by command of Wandering Spirit and found much secret gratification in braving the war chief's fury.

Wandering Spirit, sensing the tenseness in the air and dreading an outbreak, hurried round the lodges, humiliating himself, with humble apologies to the Wood Cree chiefs.

"He goes only to the fort," he said, "and will give her back. He is of those pitied by Manito— a fool. So why should I bring shame on myself by killing him? Let the miserable one live!"

That Oskatask had his friends among Big Bear's men may not have been without its effect on the war chief's inclinations. He returned to his own side of the camp.

Five minutes later a young man of Cut Arm's band rode swiftly away in the direction taken by Oskatask. Immediately afterward the chief himself came round among the lodges.

"Stay inside and have your guns ready," said Cut Arm quietly to the inmates. "The young man has gone after the mare. If he shoots Oskatask he will shout when he enters the camp: '*Nipahow!— I have killed him!*' It is the war cry. Rush straight at the lodges of the Plain Crees. Shoot them as they run out. Drive them into the river!"

Louis Patenaude was away, scouting toward Battleford. He had left me a gun and asked me to watch his horses. The Wood Crees feared Big Bear's band would decamp some night, leaving them afoot. I felt I would be glad to crook a finger for the Wood Crees, and avenge, too, at least one of the poor fellows at Frog Lake, yet as I knelt in the lodge with the rifle between my knees, my grip I found was none too steady. It was an anxious moment, a trying one on the nerves.

The wait seemed long, though I do not suppose more than half an hour passed. Then I heard the rattle of a horse's hoofs. I gripped the rifle tighter, fixing my eyes on the lower end of the camp. At a racing gallop, Cut Arm's young man presently burst into view. Behind, at the end of her line pounded the roan mare.

Not an Indian was in sight, not a sound save the ring of the hoofs to be heard. The Plain Crees must have been suspicious, and alert like ourselves. My heart beat faster as I watched the lips of the young man, coming, with the solemn issues of life and death like an oracle behind them. But they were tightly sealed and his face betrayed nothing. Onward he swung, straight through the centre of the camp. And then he stopped, before the door of Gladieu's lodge, slipped to the ground and handed the line of the roan mare to her owner. He had not uttered a sound.

A moment later Oskatask appeared, riding with his brother a single horse. They made directly for Gladieu's tent. He flung himself off and approached the Wood Cree. Gladieu snatched up his gun.

" Take care ! " he warned. The two Indians stood glaring in each other's faces.

" '*Wus!* I spit on you ! " sneered Oskatask. " Let me get her again and try to take her ! "

" My gun will do my spitting ! " retorted Gladieu. " Try to take her, crow ! "

They waited, each for the first offensive move from the other, and I, watching, thought I might yet find use for my gun. But meanwhile several of Big Bear's men had hurried over; they seized Oskatask and dragged him off. Cut Arm's young man had found the mare, when he arrived, outside the fort. Oskatask was inside.

THE THIRST DANCE: *The Torture.*

Facing p. 169.

CHAPTER XXI

To restore harmony and avert the impending rupture between the factions, Big Bear's band now proposed a Thirst Dance. This is a fête of propitiation or sacrifice and rejoicing held as soon in spring as the poplars are in full leaf. It corresponds to the Sun Dance of the Sioux, at which braves are made. The devotees dance for three days without food, sleep or drink and the young men aspiring to rank thereafter as warriors undergo The Torture. With slits cut in his chest connected by thongs to the centre-pole of the lodge, the ambitious young brave dances and throws himself against them until the flesh breakes and frees him. This may take a day; perhaps more.

We were camped at Frenchman's Butte, a high conical hill twelve miles east of Fort Pitt, when on the morning of May 25th both the Plain and Wood Cree bands joined in the building of the Thirst Dance lodge. Some went a short distance into the woods and with due observance of prescribed formalities, which included shooting into the trunk, chopped down and stripped of its limbs a large poplar, leaving only a few mutilated branches near the top to support the upper ends of the poles which would form the rafters of the lodge. Then they tied ropes to the tree and each with a young squaw mounted behind him, came at a gallop, yelling and firing their guns, trailing the tree, to the centre of the camp. A hole had been dug to receive it and in this the poplar was formally planted. The women dismounted and the bucks returned to the woods, cut smaller poplars and dragged them in. A row of posts was next sunk in a circle, perhaps thirty feet across, around the tall centre-post. The butts of the smaller trees were lashed to a rail laid on the circular line of posts and their tops lodged among the forks near the top of the centre-pole, forming the rafters of a rude sort of hut shaped like a bee-hive. A roof of leafy branches was next laid, the spaces between the encircling posts were enclosed in the same way, one opening only being left for a door; a portion of the interior was partitioned off into stalls with the same leafy branches for the devotees, the roof and centre-post were decorated with streamers of coloured calico, a sacrifice to the gods, and the structure was complete.

Before the ceremonies began the older warriors engaged in some minor formalities that interested me only a little less than the Thirst Dance itself. These took place in the morning, in the open, and constituted an exhibition of Indian methods of warfare. A pile of poplar brush was collected in a slight hollow in the centre of the camp. The women, children, a few of the whites and the non-participants generally stood looking on.

In a few minutes the painted face of Wandering Spirit appeared just over the top of a small rise. He held a field glass which he raised to his eye, looking in the direction of the brushpile; then he beckoned behind him with the other hand. He crept over the top of the ridge, followed by half a dozen others, to each of whom in turn he handed the field glass. A hurried and whispered consultation followed, they disappeared over the ridge and shortly reappeared at a different point. Then Dressy Man

—as thorough a savage as ever donned war paint but whose face nevertheless betrayed as strongly as ever face did an Irishman among his forebears—stole toward the brushheap with a knife in his teeth, pausing every foot or two as if to listen. He reached the hollow, placed his ear beside an imaginary tepee, cut an imaginary circle in the wall, buried the blade in the heart of an imaginary foe sleeping tranquilly inside, removed the fictitious scalplock noiselessly and then as quietly made his retreat.

Then suddenly the whole of the pretended war-party sprang to its feet and with whoops, cries and volleys from its guns rushed upon the doomed pile of brush. This was the signal for the crowd to do likewise, and the women and children flung themselves with the warriors upon the heap and tore it to pieces, each bearing off triumphantly a trophy in the form of a leafy twig. The whole was a dramatic play, one of the most novel I have ever seen. New York or London have nothing like it.

Afterward they gave exhibitions of fighting on horseback, circling and riding furiously; of fighting in rifle-pits hastily dug with their knives in bare open ground when surprised on the plains ; and of stealing horses from their hereditary enemies, the Blackfeet.

Stanley Simpson and I watched from a small knoll near by the building of the Thirst Dance lodge. An Indian came up smiling, seized our wrists and led us toward the structure. The long rafter-poles were green and heavy and they had an original device for raising them. Two slight dry poles were lashed together near the top, the upper end of the rafter was placed in the fork thus formed, two men took hold of the long ends of the lifting poles and raising the top of the rafter dropped it in the forks formed by the mutilated branches of the big centre-pole of the lodge. As each rafter settled in its designated place a chorus of approving yells came from the construction party.

Of these Wandering Spirit was one, and when Simpson and I arrived the Indians seemed at a loss, thinking we would not understand what was wanted of us.

"*Nisheetotumuk! Nisheetotumuk!* They understand! They understand!" cried the war chief. And he went on to tell us good-humouredly in Cree that we had been honoured by an invitation to assist them in raising the rafters. Whatever we may have felt, we tackled the job with a will and whooped as long and as wildly as did any of the redskins as the rafters went home.

Toward sundown the dance began. One of a number of young men who aspired to the distinction of a brave climbed to the top of the centre-pole and perching himself among the forks started a dolorous chant. It was a part of the rites. He was expected to sit there until morning, chanting without cessation his melancholy music. The devotees gathered and were shut up, each in his separate cell, only their heads being visible. Each held between his lips the wing bone of a wild goose, aboriginal pipes of Pan, on which they blew in chorus as they bobbed monotonously up and down in time to the chant of the drummers grouped near the fire in the centre of the lodge, the shuffle of their feet and the measured boom of the drum.

Louis Patenaude had returned that day from his scout. He brought with him a small pinto stallion, which he had hobbled and turned out behind his lodge to graze with his other horses. Louis was tired and delegated to me the job of watching his ponies that night.

I wore moccasins in the camp, and as I became familiar with the life and customs of the Indians, stalked in the evenings among the bucks, a blanket wrapped closely about me, indistinguishable from one of themselves. It is against etiquette for one Indian to intercept another strolling through the camp at night with a blanket trailing to his heels and folded about his head so that only an eye is visible. Besides, it is dangerous. The stroller may be on his way to call on his challenger's wife, or the wife of some other Indian, and he may resent having his identity disclosed. In that event he is likely to show quick disapproval of inquisitiveness; his interceptor may receive a tap on the skull from the barrel of the gun hidden beneath his blanket that will effectually knock all curiosity out of him. I took a good deal of satisfaction in wandering round among the cut-throats and listening to their councils, knowing that not one of them, while he might suspect me as the prowler, would dare to draw the blanket from my face for fear of a mistake which would bring upon his own head the wrath of another of the band and his gun.

Louis had loaned me his rifle and closely blanketed I went in the direction of the dancing lodge. The dancers in their booths jerked tediously up and down to the shrilling of their goose-bone whistles, the braves at the fire danced and boasted in turn of their exploits against the Blackfeet, overhead the young would-be warrior droned his dirge-like chant. Weird, fantastic, spectral, speaking of the primitive, the forgotten past, it all seemed in the night, the hushed embracing wilderness, the red glow of the camp fires.

I saw it all and after a walk through the camp I returned to Patenaude's lodge and with the rifle under my arm and the blanket folded about me, lay down beneath a cart to sleep.

It was a glorious night—the air soft and balmy, not a cloud flecking the high dome of the sky in which the pale May moon rode majestically, flooding the scene with mellow light. Behind the dancing lodge towered the lofty Butte of the unlucky Frenchman, its poplared sides glancing through all their leaves in the shimmering effulgence.

I lapsed into unconsciousness. But suddenly, I don't know how much later, the sound of the horses blowing their nostrils came to me. I got up and walked off into the scrub to drive them nearer to the tent. I knew Patenaude's other horses and they knew me, but I had yet to make the acquaintance of the pinto stallion. He was rather pretty to look at, with his neat limbs and creamy satin skin, but he introduced himself to me in a manner which even now as I recall it I am not sure I have ever completely forgiven.

I remember that I was not more than half awake. Drowsiness weighed my eyelids down. Otherwise I expect I should have been more careful. I picked up a small willow and going round the horses turned them toward the lodge. The pinto, front feet roped together, was slow. I struck him two or three smart taps on the rump with the switch. Then I woke up.

I saw his heels in my face. I leaped back; threw up my arm. The hoofs struck it down. He followed me, racing backward like a crab, and next—I was still frenziedly retreating—a pile-driver caught me fairly in the mouth.

The stars had been almost drowned in the splendour of the moonlight, but they now blazed suddenly forth with startling brilliance. I saw constellations I had never before heard of and an immense number of meteors. A little later I realized that I was lying stretched on the grass with something in my mouth the shape and consistency of a hard-boiled egg. My upper lip was swollen, cut and bleeding profusely. The swelling interfered seriously with mastication for some days. My beauty was marred, though not I hope permanently. The hoof had somehow missed my teeth and I have them all yet.

I have been kicked severely by several horses, but never as I was kicked by that rapid-fire, back-action pinto. He was the most energetic and surprising kicker I ever encountered. I got even with him a day or two later, when while I was cinching a pack on his back he tried to take me at a second disadvantage. I happened on this occasion to be awake and remonstrated with my boots. My feet were in action this time instead of his.

I drove the horses close to the lodge and lay down again. It was toward morning—daybreak comes early in May on the Saskatchewan and this was the 26th—and I had hardly begun to lose consciousness when I was roused by the voice of an Indian crier. Posted on the high Butte at the foot of which lay the camp, as dawn came he had sighted on the ground above Fort Pitt, fifteen miles away, a group of white tents. It was General Strange with the Alberta Field Force, looking for Big Bear.

Instantly all was excitement. The Indians tumbled out of their lodges, caught up their horses and began to prepare for flight and battle. The Thirst Dance ended abruptly, the would-be warrior left his tuneful perch. Wandering Spirit appeared riding the tall grey mare, her sides streaked with paint, eagle plumes floating from her tail and foretop. Naked except for his breechclout and moccasins, his curling black hair tossing in the wind, his strange eyes flashing, at a mad gallop he circled the camp, shouting the long war-cry of the Crees. He was belted with cartridges; across his chest like the sash of some military order hung a second band. He carried the Winchester without which he never left his lodge.

Breakfast forgotten, the Indians feverishly struck their tents, and with belongings thrown into carts and on the backs of ponies and dogs, hurried away to the east. In the midst of the excitement Wandering Spirit came with another Indian and marched Henry Quinn, Halpin and other white prisoners to the dancing lodge. I feared mischief, but the war chief was concerned only in seeing that no attempt at escape was made and left them there under a guard. I was not bothered; evidently he surmised that Patenaude might object to his taking charge of me.

At the Little Red Deer River, a deep coulee two miles from the Butte, camp was made and a meal cooked. It was then noon. An Indian took me off to mend his buckboard. My job from his point of view was a poor one, for it was not of much use to him afterward. As we were finishing dinner a red-coat scout was reported on the rim of the coulee and pandemonium reigned again. Patenaude ordered me to get his horses, which had wandered off to feed, and though I did not like it I complied.

Indians, including Wandering Spirit, rushed past me naked and shouting war-cries; they were apt to act on impulse in spasms of excitement. However, I was not molested. We hooked up again, moved down the coulee to some timber across the sluggish creek or muskeg that trickled through it and camped for the day.

Here the Indians prepared to make a stand. They went over their rifles and selected a position along the brow of the bank above us opposite the point at which we entered the coulee. It was an anxious and thrilling period for the prisoners. We could have shouted, but the slightest sign to betray the delight we felt would have been our undoing. At last! Help, after two months of nerve-racking strain, hardship and the hope deferred that makes the heart sick, was near. Often we had despaired of living through to the end of it, but we knew now that unless our captors should decide at the last moment to wreak vengeance upon us, our release was at hand.

That evening, as Mr McLean, James K. Simpson and myself sat with Louis Patenaude and several other Indians in the lodge, Wandering Spirit lifted the flap and entered. His face looked black and forbidding and as he spoke he rested his rifle across his knees. He had been told, he said, that we planned to make our way to the soldiers that night; we were to get terms for the Indians from the soldier chief. He warned us that he meant to fight; there was no truce for him with the soldiers. If we made any such attempt, we would pay with our lives.

There was nothing possible for us, we saw, but to wait.

M

CHAPTER XXII

MEEMINOOK

WHEN in the early spring of '84, on my way down the Saskatchewan with a trading outfit I first happened across Meeminook, he was I thought one of the finest types of the pure Indian I had ever seen. It was at Victoria. He lived at Saddle Lake, thirty-five miles to the east, and I was going his way. The trail was new to me, and when he volunteered to keep me company I was more than pleased. He had the figure of a senator of ancient Rome—tall, graceful, commanding; strong intellectual features; a nose with a classic bend; a voice deep, sonorous and musical.

Stretched in the beguiling glow of our camp fire late into the night, smoking and swallowing frequent draughts of strong black tea out of the sooty two-quart copper pail, we lay. And Meeminook

> " Fought all his battles o'er again ;
> And thrice he routed all his foes,
> And thrice he slew the slain."

He told of war parties, of Blackfeet scalps won in battle; of camps raided and horses run off in the dark.

" *Eigh, N'Chawamis,*" he said regretfully in his flowing Cree and grave deliberate way, " that was a time to live ! When the buffalo were like grass on the plains and with your ear to the ground you could not sleep for the thunder of their hoofs. A time

of feasting and of fighting, a time to make warriors !
They are gone now to the Sand Hills—all gone.
And the men, too—they have followed them, except
here and there one of the old eagles of the Crees ! "

When he arrived with the Saddle Lake band in
Big Bear's camp shortly after the massacre, Meeminook at once looked me up.

" *Eigh, N'Chawamis !* " he exclaimed, pressing
my hand warmly. " I was glad when I heard they
had not killed you. While I am in the camp,
Kahpaypamahchakwayo if he loves his life will be
careful how he looks at you ! " And Meeminook
remained one of my staunchest defenders throughout
the dreary two months that followed.

The night we camped in the coulee I saw
Meeminook, his face smeared with vermilion and
yellow ochre, leave his lodge buckling on his
cartridge belt. I asked where he was going—the
reason of the paint.

" To the fort." He stood looking down at me
with his engaging friendly smile, his fine eyes
dancing, took my hand and pressed it. " If I do
not come back—well, what of it ? It is what comes
to us all some time. Remember always, Meeminook
was your friend ! "

He sprang to the saddle of the restless black
stallion—the same Henry Quinn had ridden at
Pitt—and dashed after the party already climbing
the slope behind the camp. They passed over the
top and the trampling of their horses grew faint
and fainter until it died away in the night.

It happened that at about the time the war party
left Frenchman's Butte, Major Steele, in General
Strange's camp at Pitt, was instructing his bugler

to blow " Boots and Saddles " for the information of his particular branch of the command, the scouts. The major was lining up a little war party of his own. His men had discovered the body of poor Cowan that afternoon on the hill above Pitt, with his heart on the point of a stick planted in the sod beside him. Now they were anxious to find somebody not dead who had not been a friend to the murdered scout.

Pipestone Creek is not much of a stream to be invested with so deep and wooded a valley as it tumbles down.

The Indians had just reached its eastern bank and were about to descend and cross, when the ring of steel striking the rocks in the bed of the shallow stream below came to them. They drew back into the shadow of a poplar bluff a hundred yards from the brow of the bank and waited.

The scouts filed slowly by twos up the trail leading out of the valley, Major Steele ahead. As his broad shoulders rose above the level of the plateau across which the Indians were halted in the darkness, the whinny of a cayuse struck his ear. He gave a sharp order in an undertone and the scouts closed up quickly and extended in some bushes along the edge of the bank.

Meeminook's horse was a racer. When he had his head he fairly flew. He had it now. Out from the shadow of a dark cloud broke the peaceful moon, and simultaneously, from the shadow of the green bluff and across the intervening space in half a dozen bounds shot the black stallion. A shrill war-cry cut the night's stillness and echoed along the deep forest-flanked valley of the Pipestone—

with dark eyes fixed on the officer's scarlet tunic, Meeminook was riding down on Major Steele.

"*Crack! Crack!*"

Smoke puffed in his face and two bullets whisked past the major's nose. His arm flew out and two answering reports came from the Colt in his hand.

Meeminook had partly reined in his horse, perhaps with a view to a better aim. But Meeminook had aimed his last; he would never point a gun any more. With a bullet through his neck, he sagged down in his saddle and tumbled to the earth.

I did not see Meeminook again but was told that one of the scouts—who should have known better—carried about with him in his waistcoat pocket an ear of the brave redskin. Knowing Meeminook as I did, I felt that his poor body merited more humane treatment. Savagery is not altogether a trait of the red man.

CHAPTER XXIII

THE BATTLE OF FRENCHMAN'S BUTTE

I was awakened early by the voice of an Indian. He rode up and down through the camp in the half-light before the dawn.

" *Waniska!* *Waniska!* " he cried. " Twenty went to the fort last night. Two have not come back ! "

One of course was Meeminook. The other turned up later afoot. Steele's men had captured his horse.

It was a dismal note in the ears of the Indians. The day of accounting had arrived. Despite my lacerated lip, I ate breakfast in a state bordering on intoxication—an intoxication of cheerfulness. The frightful monotony of our lives for two months—even danger becomes monotonous if you are exposed to it for long enough—was to be smashed; at least there would be fighting and in the end some of us, at all events, would probably be living and safe and imbecilely happy in consequence.

The date was May 27th. The sun rose over the wooded slope behind us strong and warm, flooding the valley with its genial radiance. Little Poplar, reminding me of Yankee Doodle in his tightly-buttoned waistcoat, breechclout, moccasins, and stiff felt hat with a feather stuck in the side, came through the camp, his brown muscular legs and arms bare, his face gaudy with red and yellow paint. His rifle rested carelessly across his horse's withers. Always the dandy of the camp, he looked no less the dandy in warrior undress, walking his horse up and down, nonchalantly quavering a Crow war-song. He laughed, too, now and then somewhat contemptuously, and presently he ceased singing and called so that the whole camp might hear:

"*Ai-waik-ekin!* I'm astonished! Here are the white soldiers! I thought the Wood Crees were brave, but they do nothing to prepare to fight, sitting in the lodges with the women. Will they be knocked on the head like rabbits? Does the sight of a few redcoats make them sick?"

The Plain Crees were already stripping for battle, painting their bodies, and after Little Poplar's taunt the Wood Indians were not slow in following their example. Some of the half-breeds, too, appeared painted, with guns in their hands and handkerchiefs tied around their heads to increase their resemblance to the Indians.

Carts were abandoned. Loading their effects on the ponies and dogs, the Indians moved up a wooded ravine running at right angles into the valley behind the camp. The upland was thickly forested almost to the brink of the valley on the east, and along the summit and in the ravine the Indians began hastily to dig rifle-pits, a work in which some of the prisoners were compelled to assist.

I packed Patenaude's horses, including the devastating pinto, but I was not called on to build pits. We moved on up the slope, perhaps two hundred yards back from the valley. Before quitting the old camp Mr. McLean wrote on the fly-leaf of a book he had picked up somewhere and left in one of the tents the following note:

"Look for us north-east from here. We are all well. May God protect us."

Scouts reported the troops advancing toward Frenchman's Butte. Patenaude and a few of his Wood Cree friends, having with them the Rev. Charles Quinney, his wife, Henry Quinn and myself, had drawn a little apart from the main camp, from which we were hidden by intervening woods. Big Bear's men frequently came round to see that we were still there and advised us to move nearer them.

About four o'clock our Indians told us they had decided if possible to withdraw finally from the hostiles. We packed again and moved off. The country was covered with small timber, broken here and there by narrow open glades. We were instructed to travel " *nanance* "—abreast and some way apart; thus no clearly-marked trail would be left and Big Bear's men, should be we missed and pursued, would have difficulty in following us.

We had gone only a few hundred yards when we heard General Strange in tones of thunder demanding our release. And what music in the ears of us captives was the earth-rocking roar of that nine-pounder field-gun ! We could have cheered and cheered again ; but the cheering had to be deferred : we walked on silently with prudence dominating our exultation.

An old woman began to lament, asking what the poor Indians had done that the white soldiers should come to kill them all with their big guns. Blood will tell ! She was mother to one of our friendly Indians, but did not like to see any of her nation hurt. She concluded with an invocation:

" Oh, Sun, if you are kind to our children to-day I will show you a looking-glass ! "

What Sun wanted with a looking-glass was too

many for me then and is yet, unless the wrinkled dame believed that, like a woman, he would do anything for a glance at his own face. If this doesn't explain it, her invocation remains for me an unsolvable riddle.

A few shots only were fired. We hurried on for a mile; then coming together, after another five miles we camped some two miles from the main band. We had travelled in a circle to further cover our retreat. Our Indians still feared pursuit and our evening camp fire was a tiny one. Longfellow, guardian of the missionary and his wife, went back at dusk to lie on our trail and throw Big Bear's men off the scent if they came after us. Patenaude had gone to Big Bear's camp, if possible to get James K. Simpson, his stepfather, away.

Longfellow returned at ten o'clock. Imasees, in an extremely dangerous mood, heading a small trailing party, had been intercepted by him and misdirected as to the location of our camp. After a futile attempt to follow our tracks with the aid of matches, they abandoned the search, Longfellow protesting that we were not trying to escape and would rejoin the main party in the morning. It was fortunate for us that Longfellow met the search party. The longest part of Longfellow, I have since often thought, was his head.

Quinn, as already related, had made one attempt at escape and Longfellow mistrusted him. If in a second attempt he should succeed and Big Bear's men afterward find us, we would surely suffer. Longfellow, therefore, before leaving camp that evening delegated to me in confidence the job of keeping Quinn under surveillance. Never did I allow him out of my sight, and when it came time to turn in I suggested that as we had but a blanket each, for the sake of comfort we should sleep together. Quinn was in an exceedingly bad humour. Evidently he sensed that he was under suspicion and resented it. He preferred to sleep alone, he said, intimating further that he was quite able to take care of himself. I lost patience.

" We're going to sleep together, Quinn, and that's all there is to it," I told him bluntly. " You'd slip away and leave us if we'd let you, but you're not going to get the chance. You made one attempt and just missed losing your scalp. Incidentally, you put us all in danger. You're not going to do it again. How do you know the Indians aren't between us and the troops, guarding the east bank of the coulee from above here right down to the Saskatchewan ? You think I'm watching you and you don't like it. Well, I am, and I mean to make a job of it. Now, let's turn in."

He protested that he had no intention of again trying to escape, but I would not trust him and sleep together we did. Or we lay down together —Quinn did the sleeping.

We breakfasted at daybreak. Soon afterward Louis Patenaude appeared with Halpin, François Dufresne and a few more Indians and half-breeds. He had been unable to smuggle Mr. Simpson away from Big Bear. At half-past six we again heard the boom of the big gun, much closer than on the previous evening and so the more welcome in our ears. It ushered in the battle of Frenchman's Butte, and for three hours the solemn majesty of that verdant wilderness echoed and rocked to the belch of cannon, the bursting of shell and the spiteful crash of musketry.

Our party moved off, but with no thought of rejoining the main camp to the north. We travelled north-east, until crossing a little prairie perhaps a mile from the battleground and directly in the line of big-gun fire, a shell hurtled past on the left. To me its whistle was the sweetest of music, but it threw the Indians into panic and they quickened their pace to reach the woods ahead. The actual battle was hidden from us by the intervening scrub.

At the timber on the far side of the prairie we halted for a moment to adjust our loads. We looked each instant to see the scarlet tunics flash into sight on the plain behind us, but the minutes passed and we looked in vain. We urged the Indians to wait; they were deaf to our entreaties. Louis and Sitting Horse had gone back to the coulee to watch the fight; they refused to let me accompany them as I begged to be allowed to do.

We went on slowly toward the east, cutting our way with axes through the thick poplars, and our hopes sank as the firing grew fainter, slackened and at length died altogether. About noon Louis and Sitting Horse overtook us. The troops had retreated, they said, a number having been killed. Five of the Indians were wounded, one seriously.

This was certainly disheartening. Was it possible the troops had been defeated—that we were not to be released after all ? Later we learned that General Strange's casualties consisted of three men wounded.

We camped for the night about eight miles from the battlefield. I returned with Louis and another Indian on horseback to the little prairie for provisions left in a cart we had been compelled to abandon when we entered the thick bush. The peace of the wilderness brooded once more over the land, but that from the north the faint mutter of gunfire reached us. This, we surmised rightly, must be Big Bear's men, retreating on a line paralleling our own and shooting rabbits for food along the way.

What had actually happened was this: General Strange had retired toward Pitt and the Indians had immediately struck camp and taken the opposite direction. They would have stayed to fight again, but had no ammunition to waste. Furthermore, they objected to " the gun that shot twice." It was unfair they thought of the soldiers to fire great bullets that themselves burst when they struck their rifle-pits. Kahweechetwaymot, double murderer, had had the flesh stripped from his thigh by a piece of shell. He died before another sun rose upon his bed of torture.

Wandering Spirit was active throughout the fight. He moved up and down among the rifle-pits, haranguing his warriors, buoying up their courage. Oskatask, who has more than once stalked across these pages, was also conspicuous in the engagement. Each time a shell dropped and burst he sprang to his feet in his rifle-pit and shouted derisively " *Tan at ee !* " He had been about the forts both on the Canadian and American frontiers, had watched the troops at drill and out of the maze of orders which were simply sounds to him, had pounced on and grappled to himself the magic words: " *Stand at ease !* " He found much exuberant joy in launching at the troops, who were anything but at ease in the plunging fire from the pits above them, his mock command. Later a rifle ball through the wrist took the edge off Oskatask's enjoyment.

From General Strange's book, *Gunner Jingo's Jubilee*, I take the following extracts descriptive of the Battle of Frenchman's Butte:

" On the morning of May 28th the Force was roused without sound of bugle and after a scanty breakfast, at daybreak moved forward toward Frenchman's Butte. The advance was led by Major Steele's scouts, dismounted, extended and flanking each side of the trail. Next came the main body, consisting of some three hundred men of the Winnipeg Light Infantry and Quebec Voltigeurs, while the nine-pounder field-gun under Lieut. Strange brought up the rear.

" Suddenly we came to a comparatively open space, to which trails converged from every direction. It was the encampment where the braves had held their last Sun Dance. The poles of the great sacred lodge still stood with the leafy garlands hanging from the centre one, showing how lately a number of young warriors had been made under the established circumstances of self-torture, to prove manly endurance, while the old warriors had recounted their prowess, mainly in horse-stealing and murder.

" I was riding with the advanced scouts, when we came upon a camp fire still alight, with an abandoned dough-cake in the ashes. It was at the edge of an abrupt descent, down the wooded slope of which ran the trail, leading to what appeared to be the left of their position. Streamers of red and white calico, the spoils of Fort Pitt, hung from the branches of a tree on the opposite crest of a bare glacis-slope. The valley, about five hundred yards wide, intersected by a sluggish creek, widening into a swamp, and fringed here and there with willows. The hill salient, and the swampy stream followed the outline of the foot of the slope, eventually to join the Saskatchewan, which I knew to be about five miles to the south.

" The crest of the hill was thickly wooded, and the field-glasses disclosed what seemed to be long lines of rifle-pits along its edge. They were skilfully concealed, however; even the loose red earth dug out in their construction had been hidden by broken branches of trees stuck in to represent a living growth. There was not a sign or sound of movement; the very streamers drooped in the still morning air.

" Steele and his men were close behind, but withdrawn from the brow to escape observation. The ground on our side of the valley was hemmed in with thick bush, which left little room for formation, except a small space to the right rear, where the wagons were subsequently corralled.

" Nothing more was to be learned from this side, so I descended with Scout Patton to reconnoitre. We reached the bottom of the valley and were close to the little stream, when his horse suddenly sank to the girths. I reined back and he scrambled with difficulty to solid ground. It was useless to proceed farther, as it was evident our horses could not cross there. We returned to the crest of the hill without being fired upon. The enemy evidently wished to draw us into an ambuscade and calculated that I would go blundering on with my force. I subsequently found that the attractive streamers, which I had distrusted as being at variance with the usages of Indian warfare, would have enticed us into the re-entering angle made by their main line of rifle-pits. A long and deep shelter-trench, admirably constructed and concealed, gave a flanking fire on the left face of their position, into which the trail led.

" The field-gun was ordered up and opened fire from the edge of the descent, which quickly drew a heavy response. I deployed the small force at my disposal and ordered Major Steele's mounted police and scouts to extend to the left, dismount and descend the hill to a fringe of willow bush along the edge of the creek.

" The Voltigeurs, under Colonel Hughes and Major Prevost, went down the hill at the double and extended along the creek on the right of the dismounted cavalry, and the Winnipeg Light Infantry, under Major Thibadeau, took what cover they could get, on the right again, in the willow bushes on the edge of the swamp. Two companies of the Winnipeg battalion, under Colonel

Osborne Smith, were held in support on the hill, while Major Hatton's Alberta Mounted Rifles were dismounted and ordered to cover the right flank, where the wood was thickest.

" As I rode along the ridge, an admirable view of the entire position was gained. No sooner had my men extended than the whole line of rifle-pits opened fire from the opposite summit for about a mile. But the fire was without much effect, for the range was four hundred yards, my men had taken advantage of all possible cover in the willows, and steadily returned it. Lieut. Strange had got the exact range—600 yards—of the pits, with a few common shell. He then tried shrapnel, evidently without much effect, as the fire from the pits did not slacken. Their occupants had also got the range of the field-gun with long-range Sharp rifles and the wicked ping of the bullets made it desirable to order the gun detachment to lie down, Number Two sponging and ramming home while kneeling.

" The officer alone stood to watch the effect of his fire. There was no cover for the gun, and it could not be withdrawn without losing its coign of vantage, though its position was changed once to enfilade in succession both faces of the salient line of rifle-pits. On the failure of shrapnel, a few rounds of the special case with leaden balls were tried, with no better result, and Lieut. Strange again had recourse to common shell with percussion fuses. These, bursting in the loose earth thrown up before the pits, exploded in them, killing, as we afterward learned, one Indian and wounding three others, in one of the large shelter-trenches. The enemy bolted from some of the pits thus enfiladed into the woods, from which they kept up a desultory fire.

" Meanwhile, I saw some of the infantry endeavouring to cross the swamp. They sank waist high in black mud, and even had they succeeded in crossing there was before them only the open slope of gradual glacis, swept by the fire from the pits. I descended to the position occupied by the Voltigeurs and Steele's Scouts. Being the only mounted man in the valley, the enemy honoured me with a special salute and I dismounted, not wishing to draw fire and desiring also to test the position, which could be done only on foot. Constable McRae, of the North-West Mounted Police, was here wounded, receiving a bullet in the left leg. He objected with emphasis to being removed until he had used up his cartridges on the hostiles.

" I saw that my men were at a great disadvantage, being overlooked by the enemy, who could see almost every man as he lay, while my force could judge of the whereabouts of the Indians only by the smoke of their rifles and so could effect little damage by their upward rifle-fire on men in pits who were careful not to expose themselves. Direct advance, even if practicable, would I was sure entail very severe loss while crossing the swamp and open glacis, and I determined to try a turning movement round the enemy's right. I ordered Major Steele to retire his men, mount, and make a detour under cover of the bush to our left, to see if he could find a crossing and turn the enemy's position while their attention was occupied in front. To this end, the infantry and the field-gun kept up a slow but steady fire.

" Steele reported that the enemy's position extended a mile and a half and that he could find no way of turning it with his few men. I therefore sent an order for him to return. By this time Major Hatton reported the enemy on our right circling round our rear and firing into the corral. The thick bush formed an impenetrable screen for their movements, and I ordered the corral to be retired out of fire. Colonel Smith came to me and expressed his opinion as to the hopelessness of farther advance with the handful of men at our disposal. We could neither abandon our wagons nor cross them to the other side, the force had eaten nothing since 3.30 a.m., and the horses had not been unharnessed for eight hours. Moreover, we had only one day's rations then on hand, and the affairs at Duck Lake, Fish Creek and Cut Knife made me cautious ; I did not think it advisable to sacrifice men for more than doubtful results when I was hourly expecting reinforcements from Battleford and a complete capture might be effected. Our half-breed guides were confident that the Indians would await a second attack, which might be delivered under more favourable conditions ; and it was decided to retire.

" Beside Constable McRae, Privates Lemai and Marcotte, of the 65th Voltigeurs, were reported seriously wounded. I applied to an officer of the Voltigeurs, who informed me that all the wounded had been brought up except Lemai, who would die anyway, and that the stretcher-party refused to go to the advanced position where he had fallen. I pointed out that he was responsible for his men, as I was responsible for him, and asked him if he expected me to go on the quest myself. The naïvete of that officer's reply as he turned on his heel was too funny ; I simply laughed. It was :

" ' General, I've been shot at quite enough to-day, and I'm damned if I go down there again ! '

" Under the circumstances, there was nothing for it but to accept the rôle so impolitely left me. Ordering my son to open a sharp fire of case shot to cover the advance of my stretcher-party, I went to Dr. Pare, of the 65th, who came with alacrity, as did also Father Prevost, chaplain of the battalion, with crucifix in hand to administer the last rites of the church. We found the man well to the front, in an exposed position ; and I must admit some impatience, which the good priest did not seem to share, during the confession of sin. I suggested to the brave padre the desirability of lumping the details, which he did, and placing the wounded man, under Dr. Pare's directions, in the stretcher, the party moved up the hill, I bringing up the rear with the man's rifle. The fire grew hotter as we ascended ; the rear man dropped his end of the stretcher, and I took his place. Thus General Jingo, who finished his first fight by kicking his general, met a just retribution in having to carry his wounded off his last field.

" The Force returned to Fort Pitt, to remain for some days awaiting the arrival of provisions ; and thus ended the Battle of Frenchman's Butte."

CHAPTER XXIV

SAFE !

FOR two more days we travelled, much against our wishes, eastward, living on wild carrots dug by the Indians from the prairie sod, on balls of down—ducklings just out of the shell, driven by waders in the sloughs ashore and killed with sticks, and on the little flour we had managed to bring with us. We urged our Indians to free us so that we might find our way back to the camp of the troops. They refused. Should Big Bear's men discover and kill us they would be held responsible, they argued, and they were unwilling to accompany us. On Sunday, May 31st, the Rev. Mr. Quinney held service. Camp was not moved that day, and we were overjoyed when at a council later our guards, with no very good grace, consented to let us go.

Next morning early we were on our way westward. A long hard tramp lay ahead of us; we had but one flour bannock for a dozen mouths, yet we stepped out feeling equal to any test of endurance, for at last we were free !—going to meet " our own people " after this sickening two months of privation, of unrelieved menace, of soul-racking suspense. We must have made nearly forty miles. Late afternoon found us almost under the shadow of Frenchman's Butte. We had crossed the streams waist deep in frigid water, but chilled and jaded though we were, Quinney, Dufresne and I left the women with the others in a bluff beside the Little Red Deer and toiled on. Before leaving I changed the ragged trousers I wore for a better pair secured somehow in the camp. It was in the pocket of these discarded trousers, hanging on a tree, that I left the big brass

key of the store at Frog Lake which I turned in the
lock after the massacre began.   One day I hoped
I might return to that wild and lonely spot and
endeavour to find it, but I never did.   It was all
that remained of the Hudson's Bay Company's
business at Frog Lake.

Shortly after leaving the bluff the long clear
whistle of a steamboat fell on our startled ears.
It came from the Saskatchewan, three or four miles
distant. We could not see the boat, but the familiar,
homely sound was for us the most entrancing
music, spurring us on, for it meant that help, that
friends, that relief from a strain that had become
almost unendurable, were almost within hail.

Nightfall was coming on rapidly and we were
anxious to reach the summit of the Butte before dark,
for we hoped from this commanding point to sight
the camp of the troops. Aching from head to blistered
feet, we dragged ourselves up the wooded slope
and well-nigh exhausted at length reached the top.

The sun had set but light enough remained to
show us something of the surrounding country.
We crept guardedly out on the bald round summit,
for Indian scouts if there were any about—and it
will be evident we knew nothing with certainty as
to the location of either troops or Indians—could
see us even more readily from the bottom than could
we them from the top. Under cover of the scrub,
I slipped over to the side whence, six days before,
we had decamped on the morning we heard of the
troops' arrival at Pitt.

There stood the Thirst Dance lodge. It looked
brown and deserted, for the sun had scorched its
green roofing of leaves. Suddenly I made out two
mounted men swiftly circling the lodge. I beckoned

to Dufresne. He joined me. I pointed to the riders and the half-breed started.

" Indians ! " I whispered. " No Redcoats. See their clothes ! "

Dufresne stared. " Sure ! " he returned. " Big Bear's men, I guess. Indians sure."

We crept back and told Quinney. All day we had tried to induce him not to expose himself needlessly, against the possibility of Indian prowlers in our vicinity, but without success. Now he lost his head completely.

" They're white troops, not Indians ! " he cried. " We are saved ! "

He was deaf to Dufresne and me. He pulled a white handkerchief from his pocket, rushed out on the bare summit and waved it, shouting like a madman. Another rider tore along the bushes at the foot of the slope. I pointed him out to Dufresne.

" Yes," he muttered. " And see the squad drawn up in the shadow of the bluff yonder ! Just the size—Big Bear's warriors ! "

I looked at Quinney—and I would be ashamed to say with what bitterness just then. To think that after all we had come through, with safety almost within our grasp, fate, her tool this madman and his blundering perversity, should step between us and the goal ! We were trapped. We were under no illusion. We had been told, often enough and bluntly enough, the penalty that would follow any attempt at escape. And we were in no doubt, Dufresne, the half-breed, and I, as to the identity of the men even then, probably, crawling towards us up the slope to shoot us down.

Dufresne only was armed. He walked to the centre of the open space and stood with his gun in

his hands, waiting. " Well, you can only die once,"
he said grimly.

I went toward him, but he asked me to keep away
and I did. He had Cree blood in his veins. We should
surely be killed, but if not too close to a white man
he might be spared.

Quinney continued to shout. Presently an answer
came—an Indian yell ! I saw his face pale, but he
shouted again, desperately, even louder than before.
Was he actually mad ? A pause followed.

It was now too dark to see the group at the foot of
the Butte. A voice came at length through the gloom.

" Who are you ? "

Plain Anglo-Saxon !

Quinney fairly danced. Dufresne and I listened,
silent, bewildered. Could they actually be white
men and not Indians ?

The missionary shouted again. " I'm Mr.
Quinney, and here's Mr. Cameron ! "

Again the voice: " Well, if you're white men,
come down ! "

So Quinney was right, after all—Dufresne and
I wrong. We cheered, cheered wildly then—yelled
like maniacs. The others answered. But it might
easily have been the other way about; the judgment
of the native and myself should have been at least
as good as that of the missionary, and I still maintain
that caution, not blind guessing, was what the situation demanded.

I passed the reverend gentleman, but he was close
behind. I made fast time. Nearing the foot of the
Butte, he gasped: " Let me go in ahead, will you ? "
I could have guessed what was at the bottom of my
clerical companion's request, which I granted.

We walked into a detail of scouts under Major

Dale, General Strange's brigade officer, on their
way from the camp of the Alberta Field Force to
the landing of the steamboat we had heard earlier
in the day. General Middleton was aboard, coming
from Battledorf with more troops to reinforce
General Strange.

Our reception was overwhelming. I met old
acquaintances, mounted policemen. The major
detailed two men to accompany us to camp, now
located in the Little Red Deer valley, a mile north
of the battlefield. The scouts dismounted and made
us ride, walking beside the horses. The sentries
safely passed, at eleven o'clock we were ushered
into the presence of General Strange.

" Gunner Jingo " was stretched comfortably
under the blankets in his tent, but he sat up and
shook our hands warmly while he expressed his
gratification. He had marched five hundred miles
to liberate us and he looked his satisfaction at the
accomplishment of his purpose.

General Strange was a typical British officer of
the old school, a fellow-campaigner of Lord Roberts
when both were subalterns in India. Tall, lank,
rugged, brave, outspoken and generous, he was
the idol of his command. His striking figure made
him a conspicuous target at Frenchman's Butte.
To others fell the rewards and honours of the
campaign, but the West knew what was due to
General Strange for his prompt action in organizing
his column and for his splendid march from Calgary
to Fort Pitt with the Alberta Field Force. Not always
in actual warfare are the greatest victories gained,
and his activity had a moral effect that possibly
prevented all the Indians and half-breeds in the
North-west from being drawn into the rising.

The general ordered his cook to get us up the best the camp afforded—some meal, that ! I was shaking from chill and excitement and just before we began supper Captain Perry, of the North-West Mounted Police, came into the tent and stretching himself on the ground opposite me held out a tin cup.

"Drink it," he said. "You'll feel better."

I took the big cup. It was full of rum.

"Good Lord ! " I exclaimed, "do you want to lay me out ? "

The captain smiled. "It's all right. It won't affect you. You're too worked up."

I drank the rum—all of it. Supper finished, I went with him to his tent, which I was invited to make my headquarters. Two reverend gentlemen were also his guests on the expedition, Canon George McKay and the Rev. Wm. P. McKenzie, both of Macleod, Alberta. I think the only thing about me affected by the rum was my tongue. I talked incessantly until three in the morning—lay and talked and shook. It was like the ague, that shaking, and I could not shake it off at once. Remember, I had not seen a new face or heard a friendly voice that dared to say what it felt like saying, or heard a scrap of news from the outside world—my world—for two long wretched months. I do not wonder I shook.

Before daylight next morning a detail had brought in Mrs. Quinney, Halpin and the remainder of our party.

I do not know exactly how we felt just then. There are moments in most men's lives that, on their looking back, seem delirious with supreme joy or supreme horror. The latter I experienced at Frog Lake on the morning of April 2nd, 1885; the first at Frenchman's Butte on the night of June 1st in the same year.

CHAPTER XXV

WITH THE ALBERTA FIELD FORCE

CAPTAIN PERRY next morning outfitted me with a pair of riding breeches and other necessary clothing and assigned a horse for my exclusive use. Major Steele, with a party of scouts, was starting on Big Bear's trail. My request that I be allowed to accompany him was promptly vetoed by the general. I had already been exposed to sufficient danger, he said ; the Indians would probably recognize me, in which event I would be singled out by them for special attention. He was glad, however, to enlist me as guide and scout to his column from Frenchman's Butte to the Beaver River, seventy miles to the north.

I spent the day in necessary rest and in preparation for my new duties. Wherever I went I was an object of immense interest to teamsters and volunteers. I am afraid I found much unholy satisfaction in trying to appear unconscious of this—I was pretty young. It was, I think, my first taste of fame—a dangerous thing that has turned older and wiser heads than mine. I believe I got over it, but it was pleasant while it lasted. If I spoke to a man he thought himself signally honoured. One, a teamster, gave me a hat.

General Middleton had arrived and gone over the ground of the Frenchman's Butte fight with General Strange. On June 4th at two in the morning, a courier arrived with word from Major Steele of an engagement at Loon Lake, fifty miles to the north-east, with Big Bear. General Strange had wished to go with some of Middleton's cavalry to the support of Steele. The commanding general, however, preferred to await a report from Steele. On June 4th he decided he would himself follow the major with his cavalry and ordered Strange north to the Beaver River to cut off Big Bear's retreat should the chief move in that direction.

On June 6th General Strange moved out to Onion Lake. I rode, as guide, at the head of the column. In the evening we came upon and killed two steers ; the fresh meat made an acceptable variation from a monotonous diet of bacon, hard-tack and canned corned beef. Next night we camped on the banks of beautiful Frog Lake, and the following day saw us nearing the Chippewyan reservation at Beaver River.

I was riding with the advance scouts fifteen miles ahead of the column. We crossed two heavy muskegs, dismounted and leading our horses, the ground so soft they sank to the knees. The added weight of a rider might have sunk them permanently. Following us, the nine-pounder was dragged with ropes through these bogs by the infantry, the horses first being detached and roads corduroyed across the nasty big moulds of quaking mud, grass and water.

About three o'clock our advance party was cautiously approaching through the timber the Hudson's Bay Company's post at the Chippewyan reservation. When perhaps four hundred yards off, an Indian emerged from the main building carrying a sack of flour. He wore a scarlet upper garment and I took him for one of Big Bear's men, who had secured a few police tunics left by Captain Dickens when he abandoned Fort Pitt. The Indian mounted his horse and rode away.

Now we felt no urge to engage the whole of Big Bear's following. We were only four and there were three hundred of them. In open country we should have had all outdoors to ride over. Here there was only one line of retreat—the trail—the country being thickly wooded. Also, the trail was crooked and the Indians might by taking some short-cut unknown to us head us off. We therefore moved quietly back for a mile, and crossing a creek tied our horses in the woods on the other side. Here we were able to watch the trail and reasonably certain the redskins could not outflank us. We boiled our tea kettle over a few sticks and sent a scout back fifteen miles to tell General Strange we had located the Indians.

The sun was sinking when reinforcements, some forty men under Major Hatton, arrived. We moved ahead and near the post dismounted, left a few men with the horses and advanced rapidly in skirmishing order till we reached the open before the buildings; then broke into a run. But we found no Indians. They had no doubt had a guard and seen us when we first sighted them.

It was long after dark when General Strange came up and the balance of his command not until daybreak. We camped at the old trading post and next morning with eight scouts I went on to the Beaver River, eight miles farther north. At the Roman Catholic mission two miles from the river we found a quantity of furs belonging to a half-breed rebel named Montour in Big Bear's camp.

These we appropriated. It was like a circus, watching some of the fellows getting the packs on the backs of their horses. A white man's horse objects fiercely to fur of any sort; a bearskin is his pet aversion. They snorted, bucked and kicked; trembling with fright, and then raced madly away with the flopping packs on their rumps adding frenzy to terror. But at length we all got safely aboard and rode away to hide our plunder in the woods.

At a hut on the banks of the river a mile or two east of the mission we found camp-fires recently abandoned and the offal of a slaughtered ox. Here we turned west and entering several of the houses on the reservation secured more good furs. The Chippewyans were rebels and the confiscation therefore justified. We then struck a road leading through thick bush along the bank of a creek flowing into the river. In the soft mud we came upon fresh moccasin tracks. That they had been made only a few minutes before was evident; the water pressed out of the black muck by the passing feet was still trickling back into the impressions they left. We went on slowly and cautiously, with a sharp look-out on either side of the trail, but saw no Indians. We descended the high bank and at the river's edge came upon a bark canoe, lately drawn up. A scout raised his foot and would have put his heavy boot through the bottom, but I stopped him.

"Don't do that!" I told him. "We might want the birchbark to cross the river."

A hundred yards farther on we found a cache of furs under a small log shelter. These it took us some time to divide, and turning back, what was our surprise to find the canoe gone. So close had we been behind the Indians that they had not dared touch the canoe, but had hidden at no distance from us, slipped out and crossed while we were busy with the furs. Had we accidentally stumbled upon them, some of us probably would have been killed. However, I expect there were not more than three or four Indians and they were no doubt glad to get out of a tight corner without a fight.

Drawn up on the opposite bank lay the canoe. The fugitives we knew would be watching across the water. George Beatty, a Salteaux Indian, and myself, while the others filed up the hill, taking shelter behind large trees, remained to talk to the fleeing Chippewyans.

" Come back ! " we shouted in Cree. " Plenty soldiers are behind us. They will follow you and you'll all be killed. After to-morrow night we will cross the river."

Not a sound could we raise in response to our jibes and threats, so with a parting salute from our guns at the woods across we climbed the hill and returned to the mission, where the column had already arrived.

Next evening, June 9th, the Chippewyans, who had left Big Bear after Frenchman's Butte, with Father Legoff, their priest, having crossed the Beaver from Cold Lake six miles north, surrendered to General Strange. In the morning Major Butler and I went to their lodges and ordered the men to bring their arms and march behind us to the general's camp, a mile away. The priest pleaded hard for his misguided flock, but unavailingly. They were disarmed and the ringleaders, among them my friend Catfish, arrested. A board of inquiry, at which the white prisoners testified, held them for trial.

Next day with two other scouts I made the round of the reservation. Revolvers at full cock in our hands, we galloped up to each cabin in turn. We found no Indians, but we did discover and appropriate some prime beaver and bear skins. Those furs to-day would be worth some thousands of dollars, but lest it be thought that I made a fortune out of the plunder I may mention that the total value of all the furs I obtained, apart from what I gave away, was at that time one hundred and fifty dollars.

June 24th we started with the remainder of the troops under General Middleton, whose pursuit of Big Bear had been blocked by impassable muskegs and who had joined us on the 14th, on the return to Fort Pitt. Arriving there I learned that Mrs. Gowanlock and Mrs. Delaney had been brought in by William McKay and a party of scouts; they had been found with some half-breeds who had withdrawn from Big Bear after Frenchman's Butte and were moving toward Pitt. These half-breeds posed as loyal, but in the case of one of them at least the fiction would not hold.

This was Pierre Blondin, the man who—though as afterward developed, from no commendable motive—bought Mrs. Gowanlock from the Indians, who appeared before her in her deceased husband's overcoat and who wore all my best clothing in the camp. Poirier, whom I have mentioned before, was responsible for the half-breed's undoing.

Blondin spoke good English. Some scouts had gathered round him one evening and were being entertained with a recital of his heroic acts, when Poirier chanced to pass and caught some of his remarks. Going up to Blondin and jerking the coat off his back, the Frenchman exclaimed:

" You're the hound who would have mistreated a white woman, eh ? Where did you get these clothes ? "

The scouts were dumb for a moment; then they asked for explanations. Poirier gave them briefly and the infuriated men turned on Blondin, stripped him and dragged him toward the Saskatchewan. It might have been the finish for Blondin but for the captain of one of the steam-boats then lying at Pitt. He rescued the half-breed, though not before he had been badly mauled and was almost dead from terror. That was the last Fort Pitt saw of Pierre Blondin.

The McLeans and all other white prisoners had also arrived in our absence, reaching Pitt on June 21st. After Steele's fight at Loon Lake the Wood Crees refused longer to camp with Big Bear's band. The latter thereupon turned east and the Wood Crees, with the prisoners, continued north as far as Lac des Isles, east of Cold Lake, where the captives were given their freedom. They were all well, though several were taken ill with typhoid soon after reaching Pitt.

Wandering Spirit forsook Big Bear's band and went with the Wood Crees, probably fearing death at the hands of his followers for leading them into trouble.

On July 1st we left Pitt by steamboat for Battleford. The luxury of such a mode of travel we could fully appreciate after wading through interminable swamps and muskegs.

From various sources I have gleaned the following particulars of the Loon Lake fight:

On June 2nd as already related, Major Steele with seventy-five mounted men left the Little Red Deer River to follow Big Bear's trail and endeavour to release the remainder of the prisoners. Ten miles out a note dropped by Mr. McLean saying that all were well and the party was moving in a north-easterly direction was picked up. At noon the scouts camped, twenty-five miles out, for dinner. Canon McKay, in the advance when the command moved again, came upon and fired at two Indian scouts, who escaped. These Indians waited in ambush and shot Scout J. Fisk of the advance party, breaking his arm. The main body was dismounted and extended at once. They rushed through the brush, firing at random as they advanced, but no Indians were uncovered.

Fisk rode on pluckily without a murmur. Camp was made for the night forty-five miles north-east. At daybreak the march was resumed and at nine o'clock the advance scouts came on the Indian camp beside a lake at the foot of a wooded hill. Only three tepees were standing. Most of the Indians had already that morning forded an arm of the lake to a peninsula ahead, endeavouring to avoid the troops.

Major Steele at once dismounted his men and they opened fire on Indians crossing the ford and on the tepees. Little Poplar had already crossed, but hearing the firing he rallied the Indians and hurried back to engage the scouts. Three Indians were shot as they ran from the tepees, one the Wood Cree chief Cut Arm, a good friend to the prisoners. It was the unfortunate penalty of bad associations. Miss Kitty McLean was crossing the ford when the fight began with her baby brother on her arm. A bullet passed between her head and the child's and another cut her shawl, but she reached the other side uninjured.

The Indians were crawling up the hill under cover of the brush but the scouts continued to advance and drove them back. One man was shot by Scout William Fielders at a distance of ten feet. The attackers' rifles got so hot at times from the rapid firing that they had to drop them and allow them to cool. Three more Indians were wounded, one of these Little Poplar finished by mistake as he was attempting to crawl back to his own people. Lone Man's horse was shot under him, the ball passing through his barrel behind the Indian's legs.

Canon McKay endeavoured to parley with the enemy. A white flag was hoisted and standing behind a tree he demanded that they give up the prisoners. The hostiles answered with a volley from their guns. Mr. McLean sent by a friendly Indian named François Mellon a letter to the troops, but the messenger was shot through the elbow while crossing a swamp and had to return. A second attempt at parley was repelled like the first, the Indians shouting that they would annihilate the scouts.

At the end of three hours Major Steele, finding himself with his small force unable to follow up his advantage, ordered a retreat and retired twelve miles to await reinforcements, carrying his wounded with him. These were Sergeant-Major William Fury of the North-West Mounted Police, shot through the chest, and Scouts William West and J. Fisk of the Alberta Field Force.

General Middleton came up with Steele and the augmented force of three hundred cavalry, after a delay of a day or two to make pack saddles and travoys, reached the scene of Steele's fight on June 7th. The Indians by this time were miles ahead. Middleton followed their trail across the ford. At the farther side of the peninsula he found a muskeg nearly two miles wide. It was almost impassable for the heavy horses of the cavalry, although the Indians had managed to cross with their light ponies after discarding everything not absolutely indispensable, such as sides of bacon, bags of flour and other heavy articles. The general decided it was useless to pursue the fleeing hostiles farther and returned to Pitt.

From Loon Lake north to Lac des Isles the march was terribly hard on the prisoners. The ladies were obliged to walk, often through water, with heavy bundles on their backs. Their clothing was torn, their feet were cut and bruised through their worn-out moccasins. At the Beaver River the prisoners pleaded to be allowed to return to Pitt, but the Indians insisted on their accompanying them still farther. Although the bands had separated after leaving Loon Lake, most of Big Bear's followers going east, the Chippewyans west and the Wood Crees north with the prisoners, the Wood Crees still feared that the prisoners might if liberated fall in with stragglers from Big Bear's band.

They crossed the Beaver River on logs and in boats made of ox-hide stretched on willow withes. Stanley Simpson swam the river several times, helping the Indians cross, in order to secure tea and other luxuries from them for the McLean family. At the last crossing he was exhausted and had he not been rescued by an Indian on a log would have sunk.

A day north of the Beaver River the Indians decided to let them go, and they started on the return to Fort Pitt. It was a long weary march. They had been given a shot gun but no provisions. Stanley Simpson made good use of the gun and kept them from starving, walking double the distance of the others, by hunting rabbits. Even as it was they might have suffered, for thirty mouths are a good many to fill, but they were lucky enough to find an emaciated ox, abandoned as useless by the Indians. He was killed, the meat dried and, tough and tasteless though it was, it helped to keep life in the poor wanderers.

At Loon Lake they were met by a party from General Middleton, who had learned of their release and sent clothing and food in wagons for their relief. Arriving at Pitt, they left soon afterward for Battleford and the East by boat.

In their flight from Loon Lake the Indians forsook a dropsical woman who could not travel fast enough to keep up with the camp. Old, ill and deserted, ignorantly fearing death at the hands of the white troops, she fixed a rope about her neck, tied it to a stump and hanged herself.

CHAPTER XXVI

FORT PITT ONCE MORE

I HAD left Fort Pitt for Battleford only a day or two when the Wood Crees came in from Lac des Isles and surrendered. It was dark when they arrived, that strange man Wandering Spirit with them. Evidently the war chief saw only death ahead of him. Their lodges were pitched, the evening meal was over. Wandering Spirit came to the door of his lodge and called:

" All who wish to look on me once more, come now ! "

He went back, dropped on a blanket, and sat staring gloomily into the fire. Half an hour passed. He jumped to his feet, his hand snatched at his waist and flung out clutching his long sheath-knife, the blade struck deep into his side and he fell to the ground.

The war chief's aim was bad. He missed his heart, but cut the lung so that a lobe protruded. His time was not yet.

Yes, a strange man, this war chief; suspicious yet no coward; capable of any devilry when the passions of the savage held sway, yet kind and gentle to his family and to others in calmer moods; a slayer of defenceless men, yet daring to recklessness on the battlefield, with a record of many Blackfoot scalps. And in the end sacrificing himself as an atonement for the rest of his band. That he did not succeed was an accident.

" Once a priest always a priest, once a Mason always a Mason, but once a journalist always and for ever a journalist," says Rudyard Kipling. For journalist, he might have substituted trader. No sooner was I well out of the clutches of the savages, vowing I never again wanted to see an Indian, than I was ready to go back among them. There is a charm about the red man, with his paint, his feathers, his simplicity, his native eloquence, his irrespon-sibility—even his dirt, and in the smoke of his camp fires; the crossed and blackened poles of his shifting habitation, the sweep and majesty of his virgin land—something in all this that gets into the blood of his white-skinned brother and sticks there. It lures him away from the conventionalities, the set and fretting boundaries of civilized life, back toward the beginning of things when Nimrod was a mighty hunter before the Lord and all men were shepherds.

There were dollars and furs, bead, silk and feather work, among the Indians who had come in and surrendered at Pitt and I wanted a share of it all. Besides, there was the pay of the troops themselves left at the old fort. Therefore—I think before I was actually altogether aware of it—I found myself absorbed in the business of selecting an outfit.

This is not quite so easy as it sounds, unless you know Indians—their likes, their dislikes, their needs, what will interest them and what won't. These things I happened to know. There were blankets and print, syrup, tobacco, vermilion in little deerskin bags, butter, canned fruits, many other articles dear to the aboriginal heart and stomach, including ginger ale and cigars. I met Poirier and engaged him with his team to haul the

stuff to Pitt, and I took Henry Quinn to help me
deal it out. Then we hit the trail and in four days
from Battleford were in Pitt again. We crossed
the broad Saskatchewan with some difficulty,
pitched our tents near the headquarters of the
commanding officer on the hill above the ruins of
the old fort and spread our wares in readiness for
business. Sentries about the Indian camp a few
hundred yards back guarded the surrendered
hostiles.

I had been told by a trader who had preceded us
to Pitt, having come up-river by steamer, that I
might as well return without unpacking. He had
been there a week and had sold practically nothing.
I did not accept his advice.

Only a few of the Indians were permitted to leave
their camp at a time, yet during the first two days
I picked up both furs and fancy work and paper
dollars as well. They came with their valuables
concealed under their blankets, for the soldiers had
a way of accepting anything portable belonging to
their charges without exchanging the formalities of
yea and nay.

The third morning after our arrival Colonel
Osborne Smith, who had been left by General
Middleton to receive the surrender of the hostiles,
sent word to the Indian camp that all the men were
to march with their arms to the open space between
the two camps, as he had something to say to them.
An hour later they arrived in a body. The Winnipeg
Light Infantry in scarlet tunics were drawn up in
line to receive them. The Indians were told to pile
their guns at a spot designated and to take seats
in a half-circle on the ground some distance off.

Colonel Smith spoke. He told them they had been guilty of grave wrong in taking up arms against the Great Mother, but that the heart of the Great Mother was kind and most of them would be forgiven. There were some, however, who had killed defenceless white men, burned buildings and committed other serious offences. These the Great Mother had ordered him to take with him to Battleford. The Great Mother would say later what should be done with them. He would call out the names of those who were wanted and they must step out and take seats together, apart from the others.

He read my deposition and the interpreter called the names of the murderers—Walking the Sky, Manichoos, Napaise—with those of minor offenders between. He called the name of Apischiskoos. I saw the face of the man who had struck the priest in the eye with the butt of his riding-whip and chased on horseback and shot down a poor fugitive, take on a ghastly smile as he rose and walked to the doomed group of his fellows.

When the chief criminals had been taken the redcoats stepped between them and the remainder and they were marched down to the old fort to await the departure of the boat which should carry them to Battleford and judgment. Then the others were told not to forget the mercy of the Great Mother, for many were almost equally guilty. They could return to their reservations but they would not be trusted with their arms. They would be cared for if they were good for the future, as they had been looked after before the trouble, and now they might return to their lodges.

Wandering Spirit was ill in the camp, Miserable Man a fugitive, Kaweechetwaymot dead.

Trade was not so brisk as I wished, for many of the Indians whom I knew possessed barterable effects would not leave their camp at all. Late in the afternoon, therefore, I secured from Colonel Smith to the sentry on duty at the bridge between the camps an order, pass me with a wagon, into the Indian encampment. It was stipulated that I was to remain not longer than an hour. However, that did not matter.

Loading the remaining stock into the wagon, we drove over. In a few minutes our open-air shop was surrounded. Men, women and children handed up dollar notes, beaver skins and fancy moccasins at such a rate that I was kept busy receiving them and had to call to my assistance in dealing out the goods a couple of the more intelligent of the Indians. Notwithstanding the time limit, I was in no hurry to leave, and when darkness came, as it soon did, I drove over among the lodges, put up a small tent and stowed what little stock remained away in it. I had got most of the Indians' saleable property, but up until eleven o'clock that night an odd one dropped in with another dollar bill to make a small purchase and we smoked and talked about " the things that was " and those that were to come.

I was leaving these poor people, these children of the wilderness, with all their good and bad traits —their ready and generous hospitality for long years to the white man wherever met, until evil counsels and the white man's own cupidity and looseness and contempt brought disease and destitution into their midst and turned their hands against himself.

Many of them had been my companions on lonely trails. Some had faced danger and death to defend me. Most of them had been my friends when God knows if ever I had need of friends. I was leaving them probably never to come again amongst them, and I was truly sad.

Before turning into my blankets I walked over to the lodge of an Indian whom I had known well. He had been arrested that day for some minor offence, but his wife and brother-in-law were there. She was a woman who would have been thought pretty even among civilized peoples. She had a face like one of Gibson's women—a rather thin face with graceful lines and deep intelligent eyes. Her black hair was fine and lustrous and she had the bright coquettish ways of those women always so dangerous to men. Once a white man had fallen in love with her and her husband had gone to the white man's house in the night and tried to kill him. The white man had been sent out by the government to teach the Indians how to farm and raise stock. That weakness—for a tawny oval face—was a failing of too many of the white men whom the government employed to show the ignorant red man how to live.

I talked to the woman, telling her that her husband would soon be free again. In comparison with what others had done, he was unspotted. It had grown very still, except that in a lodge near by some women wailed dismally. I asked her whose it was.

"Apischiskoos's," she replied. His wife and his three pretty daughters, just budding into the hopeless Indian womanhood, would never see him again.

Next morning the Indians still discovered means to buy and I stayed on in the camp. With the exception of Wandering Spirit the chief culprits had all been taken and later in the day those remaining at liberty would move out to Onion Lake. About nine o'clock I walked over to see Wandering Spirit.

The war chief was a very sick man. He lay outside his lodge, screened from the sun by a blanket on poles above his head, his long curling hair resting on a pillow, his arms and chest bare except for the encircling bandage hiding his wound.

He turned his deep black eyes as I came up— and listless they looked now, but as soon as he saw me the old fire flashed into them, the fierce blood surged to his face and made it dark as I had so often seen it do before when he was roused. Did he hate me to the last? I have often wondered. The excitement upset him in his weakness; he turned away in distress. I, his enemy, had come to taunt him he thought, perhaps. I stood looking down at him for some moments.

"Have you anything to trade?" I asked at length. "I am here with goods, but to-day I go again. Anything you want you must get now."

He shook his head slightly. "No," he answered wearily, "I want nothing. Anyway I have nothing with which to buy." He looked toward the lodge. "N'Tanis!" His daughter came. He spoke with her in a low voice, then stretched out his hand to me with a ten-cent piece in it. "At least I have this. She will spend it with you."

I looked at the wasted figure with its weak voice. Could this be the terrible man I had shrunk from on that appalling day at Frog Lake ?—whom I had heard boast in the Grass Dance of the scalps he had taken ?—who had ruled a camp of savages by the might and dread of his single arm and will ? My heart was touched with a strange unreasoning pity for him. I knew that this was a sentiment I had no imaginable excuse for entertaining, yet there it was, uninvited.

"What are you living on ? " I asked.

" Nothing, almost nothing. The soldiers are good; they give us bacon and flour every day. But I do not care to eat."

" Fat bacon and mouldy flour are no food for a sick man," I said. " Let your daughter come with me and I will send you things better for you. Where is the knife—the one you did this with ? " I pointed to his wound.

He sent and got it. His blood was still upon the blade. " I will keep this to remember you by," I said.

He nodded assent and I went back to my camp. I gave his daughter jam, canned meat, tea, sugar, butter, biscuit for my old enemy. He was carried on a stretcher to the steamboat, put aboard with the other prisoners and that afternoon they went down the Saskatchewan to Battleford.

The Indians struck their lodges and moved at noon for Onion Lake. Another boat was expected in a day or two from Edmonton and I decided to wait and return by her to Battleford. I sent Poirier back by trail and toward evening said to Quinn:

" Let's go out and camp one more night among them. It will probably be the last. And I want to get Kahneepotaytayo's dancing dress."

A half-breed hired us horses and sitting that night with the Indians in their lodges we imagined ourselves once more out of the world we knew. I looked up the head dancer of Big Bear's band and gave him a fancy blanket for his dress. It was a silver-fox pelt, slit down the back and decorated with military brass buttons, plumes, bells and ribbons. He wore it thrown over his shoulders, the head resting on his chest and the splendid tail hanging down behind him. He had kept it carefully rolled up and hidden away so that the troops should not get it, but he thought he would not require it any more.

Next morning we rode back to Pitt, the steamer arrived in a day or two and we returned to Battleford.

CHAPTER XXVII

THE INDIAN TRIALS

My friend Stanley Simpson lay seriously ill in
Battleford of fever brought on by exposure and
privation in the Indian camp. I was daily at his
side, doing what I could to cheer and help him.

At length he was convalescent, and one evening
when I came in as usual to chat with him he told
me how he had been misbehaving himself in the
afternoon. He had felt quite strong and having been
bed-bound for more than a month decided to
practise a little deception against the powers that
were by stealing out and taking a look at himself
in the glass on the wall opposite him. He had been
standing before this, imagining that a little colour
was creeping back into his wan pinched cheeks
when something struck the back of his head.
He realized with amazement that it had been the
edge of the bedstead. He heard the lady of the
house, alarmed by the fall, rushing upstairs and the
poor invalid, trembling violently and looking like
a ghost, feverishly pawed himself back into bed.
Stanley was always such a modest fellow and his
landlady, poor thing, might see him in his night-
shirt !

No more experiments for a week; then we
bundled him into a light spring wagon with a
mattress in the bottom and started across the two
hundred miles of prairie for Regina, summoned as
witnesses against the Indians of Big Bear's band.

Meantime Four-Sky Thunder, accompanied by Miserable Man and a small party, had come into Battleford and surrendered to Colonel Otter. This was extremely short-sighted of Miserable Man, as he no doubt concluded when he was later hanged for the murder of Charles Gouin at Frog Lake.

At Regina I appeared against nine Indians tried at one sitting on a charge of treason-felony, among them my old acquaintance Oskatask, who questioned me at some length. I had much satisfaction in answering him. All were sentenced to the penitentiary for a term of years.

Big Bear had been captured near Fort Carlton, two hundred miles east of Pitt, about July 1st, on an island in the Saskatchewan, by Sergeant Graham of the North-West Mounted Police. The old chief had evaded three columns of troops sent out to intercept him. A councillor and his youngest son, Horse Child, were taken with him.

I was a witness also at the trial of Big Bear, though this time for the defence. I told how, at the moment of the shooting he had rushed toward the murderers shouting: "*Tesqua! Tesqua!* (Stop ! Stop !)," how he had expressed to Mr. Simpson his sorrow for what had occurred, how at our suggestion he had called a council to urge his followers to let the police quit Pitt unmolested, and had afterward held his band back when Captain Dickens abandoned the place, how he had spoken for us when Wandering Spirit in council tried to incite a second massacre, how Chaquapocase (as I learned) the night after Frenchman's Butte had started for the McLeans' tent to shoot the chief trader in revenge for the death of the murderer

Kahweechetwaymot and how Big Bear had gone after him and taken away his gun.

The old chief was in sore perplexity and distress and I spoke fervently in his behalf. With a world of trouble in the kindly expressive old eyes he sat and watched me while the interpreter beside him translated my testimony in his ear, and as I warmed in his defence and the words came fast and tumultuously to my lips he nodded his head emphatically in confirmation and the cloud seemed to lift from his seamed and rugged patriarchal face. Big Bear is dead, but it will always be a source of gratification to me that I had the opportunity of doing something to lighten the misfortunes that overtook his old age and that I made the most of it.

The charge was treason-felony and the verdict guilty. Brought before the court to learn his fate, Justice Richardson said:

"Big Bear, have you anything to say before sentence is passed upon you?"

The old man drew himself up with that imperious air that proclaimed him leader and fitted him so well; the thick nostrils expanded, the broad deep chest was thrown out, the strong jaw looked aggressively prominent, the mouth was a straight line. He gave his head the little characteristic toss that always preceded his speeches.

"I think I should have something to say," he began slowly, "about the occurrences which brought me here in chains!" He spoke in his native Cree, knowing no English. He paused. Then with the earnestness, the eloquence and the pathos that never failed to move an audience, red or white, he went on to speak of the troubles of the spring.

" I knew little of the killing at Frog Lake beyond hearing shots fired. When any wrong was brewing I did my best to stop it in the beginning. The turbulent ones of the band got beyond my control and shed the blood of those I would have protected. I was away from Frog Lake a part of the winter, hunting and fishing, and the rebellion had commenced before I got back. When white men were few in the country I gave them the hand of brotherhood. I am sorry so few are here who can witness for my friendly acts.

" Can anyone stand out and say that I ordered the death of a priest or an agent? You think I encouraged my people to take part in the trouble. I did not. I advised them against it. I felt sorry when they killed those men at Frog Lake, but the truth is when news of the fight at Duck Lake reached us my band ignored my authority and despised me because I did not side with the halfbreeds. I did not so much as take a white man's horse. I always believed that by being the friend of the white man, I and my people would be helped by those of them who had wealth. I always thought it paid to do all the good I could. Now my heart is on the ground.

" I look around me in this room and see it crowded with handsome faces—faces far handsomer than my own " (Laughter). " I have ruled my country for a long time. Now I am in chains and will be sent to prison, but I have no doubt the handsome faces I admire about me will be competent to govern the land " (Laughter). " At present I am as dead to my people. Many of my band are hiding in the woods, paralyzed with terror. Cannot this court send them a pardon ? My own children !—perhaps they are starving and outcast, too, afraid to appear in the big light of day. If the government does not come to them with help before the winter sets in, my band will surely perish.

"But I have too much confidence in the Great Grandmother to fear that starvation will be allowed to overtake my people. The time will come when the Indians of the North-West will be of much service to the Great Grandmother. I plead again," he cried, stretching forth his hands, "to you, the chiefs of the white men's laws, for pity and help to the outcasts of my band !

"I have only a few words more to say. Sometimes in the past I have spoken stiffly to the Indian agents, but when I did so it was only in order to obtain my rights. The North-west belonged to me, but I perhaps will not live to see it again. I ask the court to publish my speech and to scatter it among the white people. It is my defence.

"I am old and ugly, but I have tried to do good. Pity the children of my tribe ! Pity the old and the helpless of my people ! I speak with a single tongue; and because Big Bear has always been the friend of the white man, send out and pardon and give them help !

"*How ! Aquisanee*—I have spoken ! "

A tense silence held the crowded court-room as Big Bear concluded. The man would have been calloused indeed who could listen to that stirring appeal, the impassioned outburst of the aged, untutored orator, unmoved. The fates had been unkind. Dejected he was, lonely, shorn of his freedom, bewildered he must have been. But

however broken he might be, and probably was in
the privacy of his solitary cell, here, before the people
of an alien race who had entered and possessed his
land, he was still able to hold up his head; he was
still Big Bear, chief of the Crees. The stout old
heart still beat strongly in the warrior breast. His
spirit, though bowed, refused to be crushed. And
his plea was—not for himself; he was above that—
but for his people, far less worthy than himself
—for his children, hiding in terror, " afraid to
show themselves in the big light of day." My eyes
—I am not ashamed to say it—were wet. My
heart went out to the kindly, pleasant old man
I had known, who found " so few to witness for
his friendly acts." I was glad not to be among that
absent number.

" Big Bear," said Justice Richardson, and his
tone was not unkind, " you have been found
guilty by an impartial jury. You cannot be excused
from all responsibility for the misdoings of your
band. The sentence of the court is that you be
imprisoned in the penitentiary at Stony Mountain
for three years."

Wandering Spirit had recovered from his self-
inflicted wound. On September 22nd he was
brought before the criminal court at Battleford
charged with having on April 2nd, 1885, shot to
death Thomas Trueman Quinn, Indian agent at
Frog Lake.

" Are you guilty or not guilty ? " asked the court.

" The charge is true," answered the war chief.

Judge Rouleau, in sentencing him, said:

" Wandering Spirit, you have confessed to having
committed one of the most heinous crimes a man

P

can commit. I need not say much, for you now recognize the gravity of your offence. You were doing murder while others burned houses and committed other crimes. You could not expect any good to follow your acts. You were too weak to oppose the whites and could not have provided for yourselves even if you had killed them all, and now you would starve unless the government took you in charge. If the whites had done as you did they would have killed the Indians, but they took the most guilty ones—those who took a most prominent part in crime—and are now feeding the rest.

" Instead of listening to wise men you preferred to listen to the advice of bad men as poor as yourselves, who could not help you if they wanted to and who only got you into trouble. The government does not wish to destroy the Indians. They wish to help them to live like white men; but as far as murderers are concerned, the government has no pity. If a white man murders an Indian he must hang and so must an Indian if he kills a white man.

"The sentence of the court, is that you, Wandering Spirit, be taken back to the guard-room at the mounted police barracks and there confined until the 27th day of November next; thence to the place of execution and hanged by the neck until you are dead, and may God have mercy on your soul."

Dressy Man and Charlebois were tried for the murder of the old Indian woman—the *weetigo*—and sentenced to hang. The sentence was afterward commuted.

Miserable Man endeavoured to prove an alibi. I had returned from Regina and was present at his trial in Battleford. He was brought into the court-house handcuffed to Manichoos, another Frog Lake murderer, both being charged with the murder of Charles Gouin. Manichoos, by order of Wandering Spirit, had first shot Gouin, who had run for the door of Pritchard's house, a few paces off, when Quinn fell beside him.

Gouin was hit in the shoulder. He fell forward on his face and turned over on his elbow, groaning with pain. Miserable Man, having left me in the store just a moment before, rushed up, placed his gun against Gouin's chest, pulled the trigger and finished him.

He sat with Manichoos on the day of the trial on a bench at the side of the court-room. I stood with the crowd at the back. Miserable Man looked over and saw me. He smiled his most intriguing smile. I think he was the ugliest Indian I ever knew and I cannot imagine the smile improved his appearance. He pointed at me with the first finger on his right hand, placed the back of the hand before his lips, still with the finger extended; pushed it out directly before him. He opened the hand and moved it palm downward next his heart and thrust it quickly straight out before him. Finally he tapped his chest with his forefinger.

All of which, being translated, read: " My brother; speak good for me, Miserable Man."

I had secured ample evidence against him among the Indians of the band and the trial was short. Judge Rouleau asked him the usual question—whether he had anything to say before sentence was passed. Miserable Man was no speaker, but he did his best.

" When the man was shot I was in the Company's shop with "—he faced about and ran his little weazel eyes over the crowd at the back of the room —" with him ! " he concluded, pointing me out with his finger.

The judge then pronounced sentence. Miserable Man beamed benignly on the judge as he stopped speaking. Then in a voice plainly audible in the court-room, he exclaimed:

" *Aquisee, mahga !* "

Literally, the remark might be translated: " That's it, but ! " This, however, does not convey its exact meaning. It is an expression, common among the Crees, of sarcastic acceptance of a proposition. Its English equivalent would approach an ironical " Hear, hear ! "

Manichoos was likewise sentenced to hang.

Four-Sky Thunder was given fourteen years' imprisonment for burning the church. I secured him as a witness against Miserable Man and Manichoos and his sentence, in consideration of this service, was commuted as I told him it would be, at the end of six years.

Nokipawchass was sentenced to hang with the others for the murder of Cowan. In view of the favourable reports of the prisoners concerning him and doubt as to the reliability of the testimony on which he was convicted, his sentence was commuted. Subsequently he was liberated.

Napaise, or Iron Body, was convicted of the murder of George Dill, my former partner. He called in his defence Little Bear, who testified as follows:

" I was present when Dill was killed. Saw him

turn around and the prisoner fired at him and knocked him down."

Then Little Bear, or Apischiskoos, was put on trial for the same crime and also convicted. In his own defence he said:

" I will tell the truth about what I did and what I know. When I was at the roothouse Wandering Spirit came for me to take the white people to the camp. He went away and I heard three shots. While still there I saw the whites walking and heard more shots. I jumped on my horse and rode toward the shooting. I saw the priests already dead. I saw three whites running and I heard Wandering Spirit calling. I then went after the whites. I heard more shots. I saw one man. Other Indians were firing at him and I also fired two shots. After I had fired the white man turned and faced us and Napaise fired and knocked him down."

Napaise said : "I understood it was only a murderer that the law would deal severely with, so I went to Prince Albert and gave myself up and now I find I am accused of murder. Kahweechetwaymot shot Williscraft and then Gilchrist. Then Apischiskoos and I both fired at Dill but missed and Maymayquaysoo knocked him down. Wandering Spirit was the cause of it all. He was jealous of those who wished to take a reservation. After killing Quinn he was afraid and wished to drag others into it."

Paypamakeesik, or Walking the Sky, was sentenced for the murder of Father Fafard, with whom he lived as a boy for several years. Wandering Spirit, after killing Quinn, first shot the priest. He ran up to him as the missionary walked in the direction of the Indian camp.

" Why did you not give us news of the Duck Lake fight when you learned it ? " he cried. " You wish to side with the whites and against us—follow them ! "

He raised his rifle and shot the priest through the neck. Father Fafard fell on his face. He still breathed and Walking the Sky stepped out of a group behind him, put the muzzle of his gun close to the back of the priest's head and sent a bullet through his brain.

Kahweechetwaymot was dead by a shell at Frenchman's Butte; Maymayquaysoo and Paskoo-quiyoo (the murderer of John Delaney and Father Marchand) were fugitives with Little Poplar, Imasees and others across the Montana line; the remaining murderers had been tried and sentenced to hang on November 27th. They were: Wandering Spirit, Miserable Man, Paypamakeesik, Manichoos, Napaise and Apischiskoos.

CHAPTER XXVIII

THE EXECUTIONS

A FRAIL little mother with wistful eyes turned toward the West was counting the days until she should once more press to her loving heart a son given back to her from the very verge of the grave. I had not been East for some years. But I had known Big Bear's band before the outbreak, had been with them all through it. Now, I decided, I would remain to see the curtain drop on the last scene in this grim, emotional drama. I could not, I felt, do otherwise.

The trials had taken place in late September and early October. In the ensuing weeks I made frequent trips to the guard-room at the barracks with tobacco for the Indian prisoners. Their prison until late October was a new stable, a large log building with heavy bars placed across one end before which the guard was posted.

One afternoon, with half a dozen large plugs of tobacco in my pocket, I went down to see the Indians. I had not spoken to Wandering Spirit since his imprisonment. He sat behind the bars bowed almost to the floor, his blanket wrapped about his shoulders and the back of his head. He had perhaps not altogether recovered from the effects of his wound. He seemed lost in thought, and the face with which he watched me toss pieces of the tobacco to various Indians of my acquaintance inside was the picture of dejection.

231

I had one piece left and asked the sergeant of the guard to toss it to Wandering Spirit. As it dropped on the floor beside him the war chief started and looked up uncertainly as if to ask if I had really meant it for him. I nodded. He took the tobacco slowly from the floor, crossed his arms upon his knees and buried his face in his blanket. Had a trifling kindness from me melted the man of blood ?

Passing through the barrack square one day just before the date set for the executions I encountered Wandering Spirit. He was being marched about by the guard with others for exercise.

" *N'Chawamis*," said he, laughing and pointing to a short red-haired policeman before him, " this little fox is always barking at my heels. Remind him that we will trouble him but three days more. It is not worth while to be disagreeable for so short a time."

It was the afternoon of November 26th. The murderers had been removed to cells in the guard-room. Wandering Spirit had maintained a stoic silence regarding the massacre and the motives which prompted him to commence it—a silence unbroken even when, after pleading guilty, he had been given the opportunity to speak before sentence was pronounced.

My interest in the wild, impulsive man continued acute to the last. He appeared to have been won over by my slight friendly offices at least to tolerance of me. Could he be induced to talk, to unbosom himself to me, before the morrow stilled the beatings of his turbulent heart and sealed for ever in this world the thin, cruel lips ? I could see.

I got from Major Crozier, commanding the mounted police at Battleford, an order authorizing me to visit and talk with the murderers. I was shown into the cell occupied by the war chief. He sat on the floor, a heavy ball chained to his ankle. He shook hands with me as I took a seat opposite him.

"Kahpaypamahchakwayo," I said, "you have been shut up here for four months. You might at any time have made a statement about the massacre. You have not done so. Your followers all place the blame for what occurred on you. I do not believe you are quite so bad as they make you out; therefore I have come to see you. To-morrow will be too late. If you wish to speak, to say anything in your own defence, I shall be glad to take it down. It will be printed. Thus no more than a just share of blame will rest on your name after you are gone. Your family, perhaps, will be glad."

He was silent for a long time.

"I am glad you came to see me," he said at length. "You were through it all; I would rather speak to you than to anyone else. You could see the part that each took. You knew them all.

"Four years ago we were camped on the Missouri River in the Long Knives' land. Big Bear was there, Imasees, Four-Sky Thunder and other chiefs of the band. Riel was there, trading whisky to the Indians. He gave us liquor and said he would make war on this country. He asked us to join him in wiping out all Canadians. The government had treated him badly. He would demand much money from them. If they did not give he would spill blood, plenty Canadian blood.

"Last fall Riel sent word to us that when the leaves came out the half-breeds would rise and kill all whites. The Long Knives (Americans) would come. They would buy the land, pay the Indians plenty money for it, and afterwards trade with them. All the tribes who wished to benefit must rise, too, and help to rid the country of Canadians.

"At the time of the massacre, Andre Nault, a half-breed, told me he had in his pocket a letter from his cousin Riel, telling him to stay with Big Bear's band and he would be safe. We would never be tried for what we did. 'Anyway,' he said, 'the Canadians can't beat us.'

"Imasees told me at a dance one night before the outbreak that he depended on me to do this thing. I fought against it. I wished last winter to leave the band and go to Duck Lake. My relatives lived there. Imasees nor the others would let me go. Kapwatamut, the Indian agent, would give me no provisions. It seemed it was to be—I was singled out to do it."

He was craning forward. The quick, restless eyes burned into mine. I covertly watched the hand nervously clutching the chain riveted to the heavy iron ball beside him—I remembered he had said earlier in his imprisonment that he would kill yet another white man before he died.

"Why did you try to kill yourself last spring?" I asked, then. He tossed his head.

"I knew there was no hope for me. Perhaps, I thought, if I sacrificed myself the government would not be so hard on the rest."

He was silent again; then went on: "Will you say good-bye for me to my family if you see them?

Also to Missa Jim ? Tell the Crees from me never
to do again as they did this spring—never to do
as I did. Tell my daughter I died in the white man's
religion; I want her and her cousins to have that
religion, too. I am not thinking much about what
is going to happen to-morrow. I am thinking about
what the priest says to me."   •

I had for long wished to ask a question of the
war chief. I asked it now:

" Suppose I had been with the other whites at
Frog Lake at the moment they were shot; what
then, Kahpaypamahchakwayo ? "

He considered before replying.

" We were singing," he said at length.

This may seem a mystifying answer. But I
understood its significance. He might as plainly
have said: " We were on the warpath. We were
not looking to save life." Of course he had not
intended that I should escape; that was evident
at the time.

Miserable Man grinned at me and remarked:
" To-morrow, my brother, I am going to see my
father. That is good; it is long since I saw him."
He laughed and added more seriously: " I am not
afraid yet. When I stand on the planks with the
rope round my neck well—What time is it, that,
to-morrow ? " I told him. He turned to Wandering
Spirit. " We'll have breakfast before——" It was
easy to discover the ruling passion in Miserable Man.

" Say to the soldier chief that Manito tells me
he is not to hang me ! " said Apischiskoos, defiant
to the end. " I have killed nobody."

I rose to go, holding out my hand to the war chief.
He kept his grip of my hand.

"Wait," he said quietly, rising. "I will speak to the police."

I walked to the door of the cell and he followed. When I told them the war chief would make a speech the guard crowded to the centre of the room before him. He drew himself up with something of the old spirit; his confidences appeared to have lifted the burden of gloom that had oppressed him since his imprisonment.

"I wish to say good-bye to you all," he began; "officers as well as men. You have been good to me; better than I deserved. What I have done that was bad. My punishment is no worse than I could expect. But let me tell you that I never thought to lift my hand against a white man. Years ago, when we lived on the plains and hunted the buffalo, I was a head warrior of the Crees in battle with the Blackfeet. I liked to fight. I took many scalps. But after you, the redcoats, came and the treaty was made with the white man, war was no more. I had never fought a white man. But lately we received bad advice. Of what good is it to speak of that now? I am sorry when it is too late. I only want to thank you, redcoats, and the sheriff for your kindness. I am not afraid to die."

He paused for an instant:

"One thing only makes my heart beat with badness again!" Stepping back, he lifted the heavy ball from the floor and held it out at arm's length before him: "To be buried with *that* on my leg!"

The troubled look left his lean face when he was told that the shackles would be removed before the executions.

"Then I will die satisfied!" he exclaimed,

dropping the weight. " I may not be able in the morning, so now I say again to you all—good-bye ! *How ! Aquisanee !* "

It was the war chief's last speech.

I rose early. Eight o'clock was the hour set for the executions. Hodson, the little English cook, ex-prisoner with the McLeans, was executioner; P. G. Laurie, veteran publisher of the Saskatchewan Herald, the coroner. He named me on his jury.

At half-past seven I strolled down to the barracks. The scaffold stood in the barrack-square, the platform, twenty feet long by eight broad, ten feet above the ground, with a railing enclosing the trap in the centre, reached by a stair.

As I entered the square the death chant of the condemned red men, a weird, melancholy strain, came to me from the guard-room. A group of Cree and Assiniboine Indians sat with their backs against the blacksmith shop in the open space before the scaffold. The authorities, hoping it would have a salutary effect, had allowed a limited number in to view the executions. Small knots of civilians conversed in low tones inside the high stockade about the fort: everywhere was that sense of repression always freighting the atmosphere of tragedy. The curtain was about to rise on the final act in the shocking drama which opened eight months before at Frog Lake.

Suddenly the singing ceased and a hush fell upon the men gathered about the square. A squad of mounted police marched up, black military cloaks over their shoulders, their rifles at the support, and formed a cordon about the foot of the scaffold. Major Crozier, the commandant,

paced restlessly up and down on the left, talking
with Mr. McKay, of the Hudson's Bay Company,
who acted as interpreter.

Sheriff Forget appeared, dressed in black and
carrying in his hand the warrants of execution.
A Roman Catholic priest and a clergyman of the
Church of England followed.   Next came the
prisoners, eight in all, their hands bound behind
their backs. They marched in single file, a policeman before, another following and one on either
side each of the doomed men. They stepped almost
jauntily, dressed in their new suits of brown duck.
The weights had been removed from their ankles.
Round their shaven scalps were the black caps
ready to be drawn down over their faces. Immediately in front of them walked Hodson.   Intense
silence had fallen upon the square, the only sound
the measured tramp of the sombre procession.

At the foot of the stair leading to the scaffold
the police escort stepped aside and the sheriff,
missionaries, interpreter and hangman ascended
to the platform.   Miserable Man, Manichoos,
Walking the Sky followed in the order named.
Wandering Spirit came next. He paused at the
foot of the stair, gazing up at the structure of death
looming dismally above him; then mounted after
the others with a firm step. Napaise and Apischiskoos followed him. Bringing up the rear were two
Assiniboine Indians, the murderers of James Payne
and Bernard Fremont, settlers of Battleford.

The Indians passed through a gate in the little
railing enclosing the trap and were lined up, facing
outward, in the order in which they had ascended
the stair. The gate was closed, and while Hodson

went round behind them and strapped the ankles of each man together they were told they would be given ten minutes in which to speak, should they feel disposed. All, I think, except Wandering Spirit availed themselves of the privilege.

The elder of the Assiniboines—Payne's murderer —spoke defiantly. So did Little Bear. He told the Indian onlookers to remember how the whites had treated him—to make no peace with them. The old Assiniboine turned and harangued his companions, urging them to show their contempt for the punishment the government was about to inflict on them. All but Wandering Spirit smiled, sang and shouted short sharp war-cries.

The eyes of the Indians looking on grew big; it was easy to see how the words and actions of the doomed men roused in them all the latent savagery bred through generations. But between them and their fellow-tribesmen stood that stiff cordon of funereal capes and bristling muskets; they neither stirred nor uttered a sound. I glanced over my shoulder from where I stood with notebook and pencil before the scaffold and saw all this.

The time was up. The strapping was completed; they were bound hand and foot. A deathly silence fell. Hodson stepped up to Miserable Man, drew the black cap over his face and adjusted the noose. He turned to Manichoos and repeated these final preparations. A moment later he was engaged with Walking the Sky, who stood next Wandering Spirit. The war chief turned his head and watched him with the detached air of one who has an idle but no personal concern in an interesting proceeding. Then the black cap dropped over the face of the war chief himself and the rope settled about his lean sinewy neck.

The missionaries had sent up their last petitions for the souls of nature's savage and misguided children; a hush fell over all as Hodson stepped behind the still line of dark heads and stooped to draw the bolt. There was a sharp sound of grating iron, the trap dropped and eight bodies shot through it. A sickening click of dislocated necks, and they hung dangling and gyrating slowly at the ends of as many hempen lines. A few convulsive shudders and all was over.

I drew a long breath and stepped forward with the remainder of the jury to view the bodies. The tension was past. I had not felt it greatly during the preliminaries, but that awful pause just before the drop is something I am not likely ever to forget.

The bodies were dropped into rough wooden boxes and buried in a common grave on the hillside below the police barracks, overlooking the broad wild valley of the Saskatchewan. We certified to the death of the murderers in fulfilment of the sentences passed upon them, and thus closed the last tragic event in the occurrences of the year 1885.

The young Assiniboine before his execution asked that a pair of heavy top boots be given him for use on his long march to the Sand Hills. His sweetheart brought him some pretty new moccasins with thick soles, which he wore to the scaffold.

Wandering Spirit feared that the ball and chain of which he complained would impede his progress to the Indian Nirvana.

On a bright moonlit night soon after the executions I was twice shot at by an Assiniboine Indian as I came out of my house in Battleford. I expect he had observed me as one of the coroner's jury. For some time rumours were prevalent that the Assiniboines threatened to attack Battleford in force in revenge for the hanging of their tribesmen. Nothing happened, however, and a day or two later I left the Saskatchewan for a time and travelled East to rejoice the heart of the little mother waiting with such tender solicitude for me and my own.

CHAPTER XXIX

CONCLUSION

In concluding this narrative of my experiences among hostile Indians a few notes concerning the subsequent careers of those prominently connected with it, either as belligerents or as captives, will be of interest.

Louis Riel was hanged at Regina in October, 1885. I saw him there, wearing a ball and chain, several times during the trials, after he had been condemned. He was of medium height, compactly built, with thick curling brown hair and beard, an unusually long straight nose, small cunning eyes and hands like a woman's which he used with effect in graceful gestures when he spoke. His skin was fair for a half-breed and he possessed marked native ability, which his perverted ideas, cruel nature and overweening ambition prevented his employing to useful ends. His purpose in inciting rebellion among his own race and his kinsmen, the Indians, undoubtedly was to force the Canadian government into paying him a large sum to leave the country and return to the United States. In this he was defeated by the unexpected and rapid rise and spread of the revolt and the shedding of blood, and the scaffold was a fitting close to his inglorious career.

On my way East in December, 1885, I visited the Manitoba Penitentiary and through the kindness of the warden, Major Bedson, was permitted to interview Big Bear, Poundmaker and other Indian prisoners. They were pleased to see me. Pound-maker was a magnificent type of the American red man. Fully six and a half feet in height, he had a most intelligent face, large Roman nose, a deliberate and courtly air, and a slight stoop which gave a classic pose to his striking figure. His hair was his especial pride. It hung in two superb plaits almost to his knees. When sentenced at Regina for treason-felony to two years' imprisonment, he exclaimed: " I would rather be hanged ! " It was the expected loss of his hair that moved him. His appearance and manner so impressed the prison authorities however that he was spared the humiliation of parting with his cherished locks.

Big Bear's chief concern was for the scattered remnant of his band and for his children. He told me then, and also a year later when I returned West, the truth about his connection with the outbreak, most of his story being embodied in the foregoing pages. I had always a keen regard for the old chief and believed his word was to be relied upon. True, he was a savage, but in estimating his character allowance must be made for a condition for which he was in no wise responsible, being born to it. Big Bear had great natural gifts: courage, a keen intellect, a fine sense of humour, quick perception, splendid native powers of expression and great strength of purpose.

His voice reminded me always of his name. It was of amazing depth and volume and I have heard him say " *No !* " in tones which sounded like the roar of a lion. Yet his speech was capable of taking on a vastly different inflection, and the next instant I have heard it sink to a soft whisper, tender and musical as a child's. The old man came often to the Hudson's Bay Company's post at Frog Lake and had dinner with me and prior to the outbreak we had many times camped and travelled together. He was one of the most entertaining conversationalists I ever listened to and I never wearied of his tales and reminiscences. He could enchain an audience, white or red, whenever he opened his mouth; his gestures spoke almost as eloquently as his words. He was built more like a white man than an Indian, being short and heavy. When young he must have had immense powers of endurance.

I recall his once telling me of having been surrounded with three others of his tribe on the open plains by a large war party of Blackfeet. The Crees threw up earthworks with their knives and for three days lay in their pits, enduring all the pangs of hunger and thirst, and kept the enemy at bay. He became so accustomed to the sound of the Blackfoot bullets over his head, the old man said, and grew so drowsy that he frequently found himself dropping off to sleep as he lay with his rifle across a depression in the earthworks, watching in the darkness for the shadow of an approaching foe. On the third night Big Bear escaped through the Blackfoot lines, killing one of their pickets, and at daybreak returned with a party of his own tribe and drove the enemy off.

Had the old chief been a white man and educated, he would have made a great lawyer or a great statesman. Poundmaker was perhaps a finer savage to look at, but Big Bear was far the greater man. Poundmaker was crafty and politic; Big Bear noble, outspoken, fearless.

Big Bear was liberated at the end of two years. He returned to Battleford and died on Poundmaker's reservation during the winter of 1887-8. Poundmaker had been released earlier; like Big Bear he did not long survive to appreciate the blessing of freedom. I have a photograph of Poundmaker taken just before his death through the bursting of a blood-vessel at Blackfoot Crossing, near Calgary, where he was visiting the Blackfoot chief, Crowfoot. I have also a photograph of Big Bear taken immediately after his capture in 1885.

In the spring of 1888 I told one of Big Bear's men whom I met at Edmonton of his chief's death. He clapped his hand over his mouth—the Indian expression of surprise or incredulity.

" He always said he would never die until his teeth were worn even with his gums," was what he said, then. An Indian is usually too polite to say that he does not believe you, but I quite understood that Wapatequyoo at that moment held my veracity in light esteem. His answer was significant as showing the estimation in which Big Bear's utterances were regarded by his band. As a matter of fact I immediately recalled having noticed that the old chief's teeth were worn short by mastication.

Big Bear and Poundmaker were the two principal chiefs implicated in the uprising.

Imasees, Little Poplar, King Bird, Lucky Man and others managed to avoid capture and escape across the boundary into Montana. They killed a man drifting down the South Saskatchewan River in a skiff and used his boat to cross the stream. Little Poplar was shot a year or so later by a half-breed named Ward with whom he quarrelled over some horses. They met on horseback on the prairie near Fort Assiniboine and the Indian opened fire with a revolver. The half-breed responded promptly with a Winchester. Three bullets pierced Little Poplar before he fell from his horse, dead.

Imasees became the leader of the band of refugees, which in time came to be a nuisance and menace to Montanians, killing cattle and committing other depredations, until in the summer of 1896 they were rounded up and deported to Canada by United States troops. They were met by an escort of mounted police and Canadian officials and taken north to Battleford. Imasees, who had adopted the name of Little Bear, made a trip to Ottawa and eastern cities in paint and feathers, wearing all the airs of a great chief. He made speeches and Canadian officialdom listened deferentially and paid him due respect. Had he been captured after the rebellion he would doubtless have swung from the same scaffold as Wandering Spirit, for he was undoubtedly the real instigator of the Frog Lake massacre. From personal observation, I have shown that he was guilty of the basest treachery. But such are the vagaries of time: the accessories condemned and hanged by the government; the principal fêted and publicly honoured by the same government.

Imasees died a year or two ago in his camp on the St. Mary's River in Montana.

The two murderers, Paskookwyoo and Maymaykwaysoo, also escaped justice. I believe they are now also dead.

Four-Sky Thunder was released in the summer of 1891. I had seen him at Stony Mountain

Penitentiary, occupying a seat on the tailors'
bench. I met Peter Hourie, the Indian Department
interpreter at Regina, in the street one day.

" Did you see your old friend ? " he asked.

" Who was that ? "

" Kahneeokeesikopaniss. He came to the office
yesterday, on his way to Battleford. He said he
was sorry to hear that the *Musinageesees* was dead.
I asked him who he meant. ' Missa Jim ' *oskineku*,
he said. ' He is not dead,' I told him. ' If you
stand on this corner he will pass within two smokes
and you will see him.' "

This was early in the afternoon. I afterwards
learned that my old *chawam*, Four-Sky Thunder,
had stood in that spot until nearly train time, seven
in the evening, watching for me. I was sorry that
my business that afternoon had taken me in another
direction and that he was obliged to leave without
seeing me again. I understand he is now dead.

Lone Man put in an appearance at Edmonton
a year after the rebellion. He was trying to sell
horses, the white racer upon which he had ridden
down Loasby at Pitt among them. It was an
unfortunate indiscretion on the part of Lone Man,
for an ex-member of Steele's Scouts who lived at
Edmonton recognized the savage of the solitary
name by the white horse. He had encountered him
on the afternoon that Quinney, Dufresne and myself
found the scouts at Frenchman's Butte and about
a mile from that picturesque landmark—which
incidentally proves that Dufresne and I were
right in believing there might be stray Indians
about and that it would be the part of wisdom for
the missionary to exercise caution.

Lone Man was shut up in the police guard-room at Edmonton to await trial for shooting at and wounding Loasby. One night he escaped. He was gone for two days. It was January, the thermometer far below zero. On the third morning a detachment of police overtook Lone Man on the road.

He knew of course that several of his fellow-tribesmen had been hanged at Battleford and doubtless anticipated a like fate. He took off his white blanket and waved it in the wind, trying to stampede the police horses. They plunged and snorted but the attempt failed. Then Lone Man shouted defiance, telling the police they were dogs and calling on them to shoot and be eternally condemned. They arrested him instead. He got six years in Manitoba Penitentiary.

Whether or not Lone Man still lives I do not know, but about fifteen years ago I one day received in the mail a letter post-marked Pincher Creek, Alberta, addressed in an unfamiliar hand. It was signed:

" Your old friend,
" SAM JOHNSON."

I had known Johnsons, of course—plenty of them—but I couldn't place Sam. But when I reached the postscript the riddle was explained.

" I used to be called The Lone Man," it read, " but my right name is Sam Johnson.
" Your old friend,
" SAM JOHNSON."

Civilization do move, by heck !

Clarence Loasby has been for years an official of the Canadian Pacific Railway in the Kootenays,

British Columbia. He wears in a ring on his finger one of the two bullets received on that scouting trip at Pitt and for which he is indebted to The Lone Man.

Henry Quinn I saw several times during 1897 in St. Paul, Minnesota. He did not look much like the sprightly young fellow I knew in '85. He had lived among the Sioux for some years and appeared to have sunk in the social scale. He was big and burly and showed his mixed blood much more than did his uncle, the Indian agent at Frog Lake.

My friend and protector, Louis Patenaude, lived until recently on the bank of the Saskatchewan near Fort Pitt, with his stepfather, old Mr. James K. Simpson. Both, I am sorry to say, are now dead. There were no better men anywhere.

Kahneepotaytayo lives on the reservation at Onion Lake. Though I had not seen him since the Rebellion, he recognized me at once when I drove out to his place in the fall of 1923. No one seeing him now would believe he could have been the handsome and active head dancer of Big Bear's band in 1885, the spearer of the White Dog's Head and next to Little Poplar (of whom he was a nephew) perhaps the greatest dandy in the camp. His first wife was a daughter of Wandering Spirit; his present one is a daughter of Apischiskoos, among the murderers hanged at Battleford.

Whatever her father may have been, the daughter of Apischiskoos is a fine type of Indian woman, pleasant to look at, ready of speech, amiable, laughing and sincere. Everything about their camp on the Pipestone near Onion Lake was as spick and trim as could be when I visited them again in the fall of 1925. I made them some small presents of things most dear to the Indian heart—tea, tobacco, sweets. They were so kind, so frankly delighted over the visit that before leaving I wished to say something agreeable, something sympathetic, to mention some redeeming trait in her turbulent parent. I did. He had had two daughters, neat, attractive girls about sixteen years of age at the time of the massacre. They knew no English and we spoke in Cree.

"Your father was a good friend to me." A shadow crossed her cheerful face. She murmured something—probably to the effect that they should not have hanged him, though I could not catch it. "In the winter before the 'bad time' he came to me one day. 'My daughter is very sick,' he told me. 'She has a bad cold. I have no medicine— nothing to buy any.' I felt sorry. I said: 'I will give you some medicine. Also a little tea and sugar and biscuit for her.' He came back in two weeks. 'That was splendid medicine,' he said. 'My daughter is quite well again.'

"He never forgot that. When others in the camp were against me, he threatened them, always ready to defend me." I paused a moment: "I don't know—perhaps it was for you he got the medicine?"

Like a flash, memory flew back over the years. Her eyes lighted; she turned a beaming face to me: "Yes; I know!" she exclaimed. "It was *yellow medicine*, wasn't it?"

It was. What I had given Apischiskoos was a small bottle of honey—the only "medicine" I had had that I thought might help a cold. Across that great span of forty years she had not forgotten my trifling act of kindness. She proved it convincingly.

When we were leaving she stood with Kahneepotaytayo alongside our car with its three white occupants. I waited. They wanted, I knew, to say something, to make a little speech to me at parting. At length Kahneepotaytayo spoke:

"We are very pleased that you have come to see us. We never thought to look at you again." He was silent for a second. "And perhaps, *if Manito thinks,* we shall see you yet again sometime." And they call this man a pagan !

I have never anywhere met friends who were more unaffectedly glad to see me than these simple, kindly red folk of the Plains.

François Dufresne is interpreter for the Indian Department at Onion Lake, where the agency is now located.

Poor Louis Goulet has been for twenty years an inmate of the Home for Incurables at Portage la Prairie, Manitoba. I drop off to see him when I pass that way. He likes to talk over the days, long gone, when he could enjoy the sunlight like other people. He is completely blind.

Adolphus Nolin, vigorous and active still, lives on a ranch near Onion Lake. I spent a night with him not long since. It was Nolin and Pritchard who saved the white women from the Indians in '85 after their husbands had been killed. I saw John Pritchard at Battleford in the fall of 1925 a few days before his death at the age of 86. His only reward for guarding the white women in the Indian camp was the consciousness of a good act nobly performed. It is not to the credit of the Canadian government that his splendid services at that difficult time were never recognized. He might at least have been given a small pension, like the women whose lives he had saved.

Father Le Goff lives at the Roman Catholic Mission of Lac la Biche, north of the Saskatchewan, on the Alberta and Great Waterways Railway. Despite his eighty-six years, his health, as he wrote me recently, "is very good." The little French priest has had a most eventful life. Prisoner of Big Bear's followers in '85, he was again a prisoner thirty years later of the Germans. In June, 1914, he was in Liége, Belgium, arranging for the publication of a Chippewyan dictionary he had written, when the Great War broke. He was captured and shut up in a monastery, but escaped to Switzerland. He continued after his return to labour among the Chippewyans, with whom he must have spent nearly fifty years, until quite recently.

Mr. W. J. McLean lives, with several of his numerous family, all long grown up, in Winnipeg.

On Poundmaker's reserve last fall, I looked up Horse Child, Big Bear's only surviving son. In build and many little mannerisms he reminded me strongly of his father. He was twelve at the time of the '85 troubles; now he is fifty-two. I met there also Sakamataynew, Poundmaker's only son.

My dear old comrade, Frederick Stanley Simpson, met his death on October 1st, 1891, in the Nelson River, a tributary of Hudson Bay, in an heroic effort to save the life of his senior officer, Horace Belanger, chief factor in charge of the Hudson's Bay Company's district of Norway House. Belanger

FINE DAY.
LEADER OF THE INDIANS IN THE CUT KNIFE BATTLE, 1885
(PHOTO 1925).

KAHNEEPOTAYTAYO.
BIG BEAR'S HEAD DANCER (PHOTO 1925).

Facing p. 252,

was an immense man, helpless out of his depth. Their canoe capsized in a dangerous rapid and Simpson, a powerful swimmer, exhausted by his exertions to help his chief and paralysed by the icy water, sank to rise no more, Belanger also losing his life. The sacrifice was witnessed by an Indian, the third member of the party, who escaped. The following are the last lines of some verses I wrote in his memory at the time of the tragedy:

" Lord Jesus, Thou Who even betrayer's kiss
Forgiving, shed Thy precious blood to drown
    For ever all earth's sin, and said, than this
    Hath no man greater love, that he lay down
Life for his friend—grant him a meritorious crown."

Simpson had the nature of a true nobleman. He was my greatest friend.

Frog Lake is no longer deserted, but the centre of a beautiful and thriving white settlement. A railway under construction from Battleford to Edmonton north of the Saskatchewan will reach it this year of 1926, and its hills, which have echoed to the whoops of the red man, will give back only the peaceful whistle of the locomotive. Its isolation and wild loneliness are things of the past.

THE FROG LAKE MEMORIAL

I stood on the site of the grey drama of '85, envisioning all its harrowing details. Again it was a beautiful day. Overhead the sun shone brightly; a soft air faintly stirred the green leaves of the poplars. Indians, some who like me had witnessed the incarnadined saturnalia, stood about; half-breeds also, and many whites—men, women and children. But the awful suspense and foreboding that had weighed upon us, early sojourners in the land, on that distant day, were absent. We now here were met together in peace, although it was that unforgettable day and event that had drawn us to this common centre, for we were come to attend a significant ceremony—the unveiling of a monument erected by the government of Canada as a lasting reminder of that sombre and historical occurrence.

The date was the 9th of June, 1925. Judge Howay, of New Westminster, B.C., member of the Board of Historic Sites and Monuments, represented the government. Accompanying him were Howard Angus Kennedy, who had come to Frog Lake in 1885 as correspondent for a Montreal newspaper, and Arthur S. Morton, professor of history at the University of Saskatchewan. Judge Howay asked me, as the sole white survivor of the massacre, to unveil the memorial.

While he addressed the gathering I stood before the cairn and looked about me. Close beside it were eight graves, marked by simple iron crosses bearing names familiar to me since youth: Quinn, Delaney, Gowanlock, Gilchrist, Dill, Gouin, Williscraft, Cowan—the names of men nearly all of whose hands, long cold and still,

*had once met mine in the warm clasp of friendship.
Memory brought back vividly the faces of these pioneers,
once so full of life, of plans, of ambitions. I recalled
their ready laughter, their boisterous pranks, their
pleasant voices. And I reflected that for forty years
they had rested there ; that the snows of forty winters
and the showers of forty summers had fallen like a
benediction upon them, the caressing, flower-scented airs
blown over them, as they slept their dreamless and
unbroken sleep.*

*Across the short intervening span of wooded hill
and gentle, grassy slope I saw the spot that had marked
for these adventurous souls the end of the trail. I heard
again all those frightful sounds—the exploding guns,
the startled shrieks and outcries, the galloping horses,
the strangely-terrifying cadence of the* mauchawahawm-
nigamawn—*the war-song—and the appalling whoops
of the frenzied savages, the ineffectual " Stop ! Stop ! "
of Big Bear as he rushed toward the carnage, the
sputtered admonition of shaking old Osowask, old
Yellow Bear, willing, yet fearful too, openly, in that
hour of dreadful deeds, to befriend me : " Go with
the women—don't leave them ! " And I remembered,
too, the hopelessness that possessed me, the impossibility
at the moment of the thought that I should by any
miracle escape the doom that with such stupefying and
ghastly suddenness was sweeping over the others.*

*Yes, for forty years these gallant fellows had rested
quietly there, while I walked and wrought and played
in God's glorious sunlight and had known all the joy
of living and now had sons grown to the age that
I was then.*

*An Indian, a pure blood Cree, mounting a knoll,
read in rounded English periods from a manuscript in*

*his hand an eloquent address. It was not an apology—
it was not meant to be—for the massacre, but it was a
plea for charity, for consideration, for understanding of
the red man and of the feelings which culminated in the
commission of that dark and bloody crime. He cast what
must have been to most of the listening white men a new
light on that ruthless and deadly act of vengeance. The
land of the Indian, a proud people, was being wrested
from his grasp by pale-skinned strangers who looked
with scarcely-disguised contempt upon him as an inferior
and derided his pretensions of ownership. Well! The
Indian was not to be trampled upon—he would show
them ! He would destroy the invader ; the land should
know him no more ; he would take back his country !
Poor, simple children of nature ! The provocation,
while it did not excuse, was some mitigation of the
ferocious wrong. Let the white man put himself in the
Indian's place ! Even so, the majority were against it ;
Big Bear's men only, and a few others were implicated.*

*The speaker was the Reverend Edward Ahenakew,
an ordained clergyman of the Church of England.*

*I drew the cord ; the flag fluttered down. The cairn,
its bronze inscription glowing in the warm sunlight,
stood uncovered. The government of the country had
paid its tribute to these stalwart pioneers of '85.*

It was a solemn moment.

BRISTOL : BURLEIGH LTD., AT THE BURLEIGH PRESS

LaVergne, TN USA
05 April 2010
178239LV00004B/6/A

9 781432 566463